PAR
UNCHAINED

Overcoming the Ten Deceptions
That Shackle Christian Parents

Dr. James D. Dempsey

PARENTING UNCHAINED: Overcoming the Ten Deceptions That Shackle
Christian Parents

First printing: 2014

Unless otherwise noted, Scripture quotations are taken from the *New
American Standard Bible,* ©Copyright 1960, 1995 by The Lockman
Foundation. Used by permission. Scripture quotations marked NKJV are
taken from the New King James Version. Copyright ©1982 by Thomas
Nelson, Inc. Used by permission. All rights reserved. Scripture quotations
marked KJV are taken from the King James Version of the Bible. (Public
Domain.) Scripture quotations marked ESV are taken from *The Holy Bible,
English Standard Version.* Copyright ©2000; 2001 by Crossway Bibles, a
division of Good News Publishers. Used by permission. All rights reserved.
Scripture quotations marked BBE are taken from the *Bible in Basic English.*
(Public Domain.) Mr. C.K. Ogden. The author has added italics to Scripture
quotations for emphasis.

Library of Congress Cataloging-in-Publication Data

PARENTING UNCHAINED: Overcoming the Ten Deceptions That Shackle
Christian Parents
By Dr. James Dempsey

978-1-888685-65-7 (paperback book)
1. Child rearing–Religious aspects–Christianity.
978-1-888685-66-4 (eBook)
1. Child rearing–Religious aspects–Christianity.

Dempsey, James, 1960-

Published by the National Center for Biblical Parenting, a nonprofit
corporation committed to the communication of sound, biblical parenting
principles through teaching, counseling, and publishing written, audio, and
video materials.

You may email us at parent@biblicalparenting.org

biblicalparenting.org
biblicalparentinguniversity.com

d6culture.com

Learn more about Dr. Dempsey's ministry at D6Culture.com

Acknowledgements

This book was in the oven for a long time, thus many assistant cooks added dashes of seasoning. I'm grateful first of all to my wife who put up with me while God was getting my attention. Gail is a gift from God, and I can't thank her enough for her support for me as a writer, as a husband, and as a father. All three of my daughters experienced my parenting mistakes and still loved me. Denise Mayen, Sarah Janecka, and Lisa Dempsey; I love you! My mom and dad, Dennis and Betsy, provided me a loving picture of parenting. Thank you!

Several folks were readers of the first draft, namely Bob and Sally Anderlitch, John and Connie Welch, and Roy and Margaret Fitzwater. Late in the process Erin Brown (The Write Editor) did the heavy lifting of editing, then my sister Jan Willson put the final polish on the manuscript. When I needed a sounding board, my daughter Denise Mayen gave me a young mom's perspective. I'm thankful to many friends at First Baptist Church of Keller, Texas for various kinds of support, but especially to two friends who have encouraged me in family ministry: Jim and Susan Riddle. The staff and members of Anderson Mill Baptist Church in Austin have emboldened me to reach more families for Christ. I'm most grateful to God who redeemed me through His Son Jesus and gave me all these other family and friends.

Finally, Scott Turansky and Joanne Miller of the National Center for Biblical Parenting inspired several parts of this book, including the portions about disciplining children and the priority of relationship between parent and child. I'm grateful to be connected to their ministry.

Endorsements

Any Christian parent will be motivated by *Parenting Unchained* because looking at the model of God and Jesus inspires our everyday work with our kids. A masterful work!

— *Dr. Scott Turansky*
cofounder, National Center for Biblical Parenting

• • •

Effective parenting is not just about the children, it relates directly to the character of the parents. Parents should not just teach their children, they should live what they teach, i.e. "walk their talk." Dr. Dempsey makes an overwhelming case for this principle.

Dr. Dempsey emphasizes the importance of children being disciplined for the right reasons. In addition, children should be taught that life is not always easy. There are challenging times in life and there are consequences for inappropriate behavior.

Parenting Unchained should be an essential part of resources sought and used by parents wishing to rear healthy, stable and productive children. It will enable parents to reach the status of their children being a "blessing and a pleasure."

Without reservation, I wholeheartedly endorse Dr. Dempsey's point of view and treatment of the parenting subject presented in this book.

— *Dr. Forrest E. Watson*
Ch/CEO, Young Leaders Campus Childcare Centers
Former Superintendent of Hurst-Euless-Bedford
School District

Endorsements

In *Parenting Unchained* Jim Dempsey assists leaders and families in realizing many of the lies that are destroying their homes. In this unique resource, Jim pours out his heart and he shares from his past successes and failures. He not only educates families on these deceptions, but as I have seen personally he models and encourages parents with practical tools to build godly homes.

— *Lance Crowell*
Church Ministries Associate for Discipleship Ministries, Men's Ministry, Family Ministry Southern Baptists of Texas Convention

• • •

Parenting Unchained is a must read for parents (and grandparents). Jim describes ten deceptions that will "shackle Christian parents" along with ten truths that will help parents lay the Godly foundations for their families. In the first chapter Jim sincerely shares his personal testimony of his realization for the importance of laying a biblical foundation for his family. This book gives parents the tools to build the Godly home most desire and reminds them that "life is hard but the mission is worth it."

— *Karen Kennemur, PhD*
Assistant Professor of Childhood Education School of Church and Family Ministries Southwestern Baptist Theological Seminary

Endorsements

If your family has ever suffered an attack by the evil one (and you are an anomaly if you have not) then you need to read this refreshing book, *Parenting Unchained*. In it, Dr. Dempsey explores Ten Deceptions that Shackle Christian Parents. This book will give you creative insights to overcome those shackles and live a more abundant life through Jesus Christ our Lord who gives us all the power to *"overcome the evil one."* Romans 8:37 says *"In all things we are more than conquerors through Him that loved us."* When you read this book and learn to overcome the ten deceptions it describes, you will move into the presence of Him who is able to conquer through your family life.

— *Jack D. Terry, Jr. Ph.D.*
Senior Professor of Foundations of Education
Vice President Emeritus for Institutional Advancement,
Special Assistant to the President
The Jack D. Terry, Jr. School of Church and
Family Ministries
Southwestern Baptist Theological Seminary

Contents

Introduction

Someone Wants to Take You Captive

"See to it that no one takes you captive through philosophy and empty deception..." Col. 2:8

Did you ever have the feeling that you lacked important information? Or worse, that it was being kept from you? It's unsettling ... a little like being the victim in that game Crossed, Uncrossed, in which several people sit in a circle and pass a pair of scissors from one person to the next. I played it once. It was supposed to be an icebreaker game to welcome new people into a group. The object was for the new person to guess the pattern for passing the scissors. Every time a person passed the scissors, they would hold the scissors in some varied position and say, "I received the scissors crossed [or uncrossed], and I pass it to you uncrossed [or crossed]," or some variation of that phrase. When it came around to me, I would say the phrase, pass the scissors in what I hoped was the right orientation, and then everyone would laugh at me. I was clueless!

I hated that game. I was the new guy to the group, and everyone else seemed to know something I didn't. They knew that regardless of how the scissors were passed (upside down, pointing left, closed, open, etc.), the only important clue was whether the passer's legs were crossed or uncrossed. I focused on the scissors, trying to discover some intricate pattern, but all the while the key was the passer's leg position. It had nothing to do with the scissors!

They were just a diversion. While the game went on and on, with more and more frustration building inside me, I felt like I was caught in a trap. The chains came off when I finally learned the truth.

No one wants to be trapped, but that's just what Satan has done to many parents today. He's trapped us in lies that make us focus on the wrong things in parenting. In fact, he has propagated at least ten deceptions to keep us from parenting the way God intended. Satan deceives because he knows how valuable the truth is. His deceptions divert us from God's path and into the quicksand of error. God's truths about parenting help us stay on track. They help us raise godly children. And godly children are a threat to Satan!

In the pages that follow, I share these ten deceptions. I've experienced them all, and each one can put you in chains.

But I have good news to share, too. For each deception there's a powerful parenting truth—powerful enough to free you and make parenting enjoyable. Enjoyable? You may have resigned yourself to simply endure parenting. You may believe enjoyment to be out of reach, but the Bible says that godly children are a blessing and a pleasure. Doesn't that sound good? So here are your two choices: learn God's truths that lead to joyful parenting, or trudge on in Satan's shackles of ignorance and frustration. Think of it as a mixed martial arts match in your mind. Satan uses lies to make you tap out, to give up on Godly parenting, but Scripture has truths that will break any hold and bring you victory. Let's list both the deceptions and God's truths briefly, and then we'll explore them fully in the chapters ahead.

The Ten Deceptions and Ten Truths

1. **Satan wants you to think that it's all about your kids—your character doesn't matter. But God says your character is the foundation for your parenting.** Your character ultimately depends on your relationship with God through Christ.

2. **Satan tells parents** that they can handle life's problems in their own strength. The lie sounds like this: **You're capable. You can do this. But God didn't intend for parenting to be done apart from Him. You need the wisdom found in His Word.** If we look, God reveals Himself in the Bible as a model for parenting.

3. **Satan spreads the lie that God cares only about rules. But parenting in God's model requires a love relationship.** Old and New Testament stories affirm God's focus on relationships over and above rules. Parents must take the initiative to build a loving relationship with their children.

4. **Satan wants you to believe that you don't need to invest much time in your children. But the truth is that God-modeling parents share life with their children.** God was intimate with Israel in its early stages through the drudgery of a desert journey and the stresses of battle. Jesus taught his disciples through years of living life in their presence.

5. **Satan wants you to believe that teaching the right information is enough, but God modeled what He taught.** God gave the perfect Law, teaching us the right information. But He didn't stop there. He sent Jesus to live it out perfectly. We too must live out what we say, steering clear of hypocrisy.

6. **Satan says that why and how we discipline don't matter (just make them obey), but God disciplined His children in ways that touched the heart.** Human parents most often focus on outward behavior as we discipline our children, but God always cares more about the heart—what Scripture calls the inner man. God uses a variety of discipline methods to achieve specific purposes.

7. **Satan says that you don't have to talk about your faith. But God taught truth directly and diligently.** Satan will tempt you to assume your children are learning right from wrong as they see you live. But God gave us the Bible—specific instructions—with extensive attention to the details of life so that we would not lack understanding. Jesus, too, explained His teachings thoroughly to train the hearts of his disciples.

8. **Satan says that children should choose what to do with their lives; therefore, you don't need to help them see their mission. But God gave His children a mission and prepared them for it.** God prepared Israel, and Jesus methodically prepared His disciples for a mission. Parents must prepare their children to launch into God's world.

9. **Satan says good parenting is all about consistency. But God adapted His methods and relationship with His children.** Consistency taken to an extreme becomes a rut. Through clear shifts in teaching, God led Israel in different ways through the years. Jesus intentionally changed his tactics over the course of His ministry as He armed his disciples for independent maturity.

10. **Satan has convinced parents that life should be**

easy for their children. This is an especially damaging lie because when life becomes difficult and Christian youth aren't prepared for the challenge, they leave the faith. In our modern age of convenience, tough times can cause Christians of any age to doubt. God never promised His children that life would be easy. In fact, **God sends His children into a hostile world with a life-or-death mission.** But God goes with them to empower, help, and protect.

How Can Reading *Parenting Unchained* Help?

If you haven't figured it out already, Satan is a liar. And if parenting is important to God, rest assured that Satan wants to deceive parents and disrupt the transmission of their faith. Satan wants you to take your eyes off of the most important aspects of parenting and put your focus on trivial or even destructive things. *Parenting Unchained* helps you keep the most important principles of parenting in mind while avoiding Satan's traps. It gives you insight to make important educational and child-care decisions, and it reminds you of the importance of simply being present. *Parenting Unchained* explains the biblical motives for modeling, discipline, and instruction, illuminating the methods that Jesus, the Master Teacher, used. It teaches you how to help your children find their ultimate purpose in life and lays out the three final steps that will launch your children toward their unique futures.

The family is God's idea, and He intends it to be a setting for disciple making. The family is the bridge to the next generation of disciples. Sadly, this bridge is cracking under the weight of prodigal children and their discouraged parents. Satan has played a leading role in this devastation by telling lie upon lie. *Parenting Unchained* will help you break Satan's chains so you can lead your children to lay a foundation of faith.

Deception 1:
It's All About Your Kids;
Your Character Doesn't Matter

Chapter One
The Foundation for Parenting

Satan's first deception strikes at the foundation of parenting. If you listen to him, he'll tell you that *parenting is all about your kids. It's not about your character.* Satan wants you to think that parenting is *only* about your kids. He wants you to see what's wrong with them but ignore what's wrong with you. As a parent, you naturally focus on your kids' faults and praise their successes. No need to look inside your own heart, right?

Some parents caught in this deception tell themselves, "I don't need to worry about my own sins. I'm pretty much stuck with me anyway. Not much chance for this old dog to learn new tricks. I'll just concentrate on my kids and their sins." Other parents don't consciously ignore their sins, but in the heat of the parenting battle, they find it much easier to see their kids' problems than to see their own. Either way, we fail to spend time training our own hearts so that we can be the right kind of person. We ignore our own character flaws, and all we see are our kids' flawed characters.

But parenting **is** about your character, because it forms the foundation for all you do as a parent. That's the truth!

Foundations Matter — A Personal Story

House foundations rarely call attention to themselves. You might say they "lay low." (Pun intended!) After a house is built, you rarely discuss the foundation. Nobody comes over to your house, walks into your living room, and says, "Wow, nice foundation," or "Nice concrete! What kind of compression rating you got on this thing?" Still, you place your most precious possessions on it, confident that it will prop up your walls and hold up your roof for decades. But a foundation surely can cause trouble if you build it poorly or in the wrong place.

Most married couples in America, if they are moderately blessed financially, will own a home, and some even have the opportunity to build their dream homes. If they build, they will watch with excitement as their foundation is poured and construction begins.

Unlike most couples, when my wife and I got married, I already owned the foundation for my home. (I also owned a 1972 Vega, two polyester leisure suits, and a guitar.) I was rather proud of that foundation. It had been built, I must confess, with help from my parents. But by and large, I laid this foundation through my own efforts.

You may think it unusual that a young man would already have a foundation for his home. Actually, I picked out the spot for my foundation on a nearby hill when I was only nine years old and made my first real contribution to its construction when I was sixteen. By the time I graduated from high school, my concrete foundation was pretty much complete. Then I went confidently off to college. And that's when the trouble started. Somehow, my foundation slid down the hill from its original spot, cracked severely, and came to rest straddling the property line I

16

shared with an old family enemy. Now, half of my foundation was not even on my own property. Yet contrary to good sense and in spite of various legal issues, I determined to build my house anyway. Of course, I used my own property address—I didn't want anyone to know that I actually lived on my enemy's property. You'd be surprised how long you can continue to build, and how complete a house can become, even with such foundation problems.

If I have fooled you into thinking this was a foundation for a house, forgive my trickery. I needed to make a point. The foundation I just described was the foundation for my home—a foundation for my marriage. I laid the cornerstone of that foundation when I was nine years old by asking Jesus Christ to be my Savior. I made the decision at age sixteen to take Christ seriously, to try to live by His standards. And it really was during my college days that trouble began. Faced with the choice to put Christ or the world first, I decided I would do both. Thus, I built my house (my worldview, my values, my goals, my habits, my career, and my relationship with my wife) straddling two pieces of property—half on the solid rock lot that I first chose at age nine, and half on the decidedly sandy lot next door. The sandy lot represented my determination to party hard and live by the world's standards. By the way, wherever you live, Satan (an old family enemy) always owns the sandy lot next door.

As I went about my life on the rock lot, I attended church on Sundays, seeking God's will. On the sandy lot, I worked late hours, seeking the world's approval. On the rock lot, I understood that God had picked out my mate. On the sandy lot, I was resentful of a wife who did not meet my needs according to the world's propaganda. On the rock lot, I felt pangs of guilt from time to time for my wandering eye. On the sandy lot, I spent more and more of my mental energy wondering about and wishing for opportunities to be unfaithful. Though I lived this dual life in all parts of my "house," the most obvious cracks in the foundation were under the "family room," my marriage. I felt guilty but powerless to make real change. My wife felt lonely, neglected, and left out of the partnership that should have been our marriage. I suppose we tolerated this sorry estate due to the love we both had for our first child, Denise.

Then came Neil.

I knew that God would not let me, as His child, continue in sin without His intervention, but when you are sinning as effortlessly as I was, you're able to keep that sort of thinking locked in a closet. Our son, Neil, was a big surprise, since Gail became pregnant just four months after Denise was born. But great anticipation soon replaced our shock.

When Neil was born, his skin was tinged slightly blue, which worried us somewhat. But the doctor showed no outward concern. His Apgar test was normal, so we relaxed a bit.

The morning after Neil's birth I was at my office (what does this tell you about my priorities?). My wife called, telling me that something was wrong. Gail couldn't even speak because of her emotions, so her visiting friend told me to come to the hospital quickly.

My grand house on the straddling foundation trembled.

What the doctor told us rocked my safe and snug little world. Neil had four major heart defects: some features were missing altogether, others misplaced or misshapen.

Any one of them would have been debilitating, and to have all four was extremely rare. To have all four and live was unbelievable. "Imagine that a four-year-old has done the plumbing in your house. That's the best way I can describe what your son's heart is like," the cardiologist explained. Neil would require major surgery that very day, less than twenty-four hours after birth, to have any chance of survival.

Miraculously, he did survive, and he seemed to do okay for four months. Of course, "okay" still meant major medical bills, long and difficult days caring for Neil, and excruciating nights when coaxing two ounces of formula to stay down took hours. During this time, Gail and I were taking the equivalent of college courses in prayer from the School of Hard Knocks. We begged God to heal Neil. Neil's doctor told us to expect major surgery—so major that Neil would have to be four or five years old to have a realistic chance of survival. Our goal then became doing whatever we could so that Neil would survive to age four.

From four months to eight months, Neil struggled, lost weight, and grew more agitated. Swallowing a few ounces of formula caused him to sweat like a heavyweight fighter in a Gatorade commercial. Though I helped Gail when I was home, my work still required, and received, more attention than was healthy for a young marriage, especially one with a heavy dose of emotional and financial stress. While I was on one of my too-frequent out-of-town trips, Gail called to tell me that Neil was in crisis.

The house I built on that wayward foundation developed a precarious lean.

Gail had to face this grave crisis without me at her side. I caught a flight and returned as soon as I could, but the stress of those hours weighed enormously on her. Neil, his blood too thick to extract a sample from his thin arms, was wheeled into surgery with an intravenous needle stuck in his forehead. That image sticks just as painfully in my memory even today. Gail and I prayed in the hospital's chapel, and both of us felt God's comfort that Neil would be okay. Just then, the surgeon found us. He described the fight Neil gave, but his heart would not restart. It was just plain worn out.

At that moment my arms reached to comfort Gail, but my mind reeled, watching the house I had built, half on the rock and half on the sand, crumble finally and fully to the ground. Dealing with that heap of debris would later be as agonizing to me as the loss of our son.

In that splintered pile of debris lay my sheltered, distorted view of God. All my life I believed that when I earnestly prayed, I would get what I prayed for, but now the object of my prayer had just breathed his last breath. Once, I believed that God would bless me (as I defined blessing) in spite of my sin. Now, I doubted God's very existence, much less His benevolence. Once upon a time, I believed in the God my parents had taught me about, a God of love and mercy. Now that my fairy-tale life had vanished, I wondered if such a God existed. It is one thing to lose a child of eight months. It is another to lose the God of a lifetime.

I have always been one to question, and I certainly questioned at that moment and for the next few months "Is there a God? What is He like? Is the Bible a believable presentation of God, or is it all baloney, all a myth?" As I considered all that I had been taught, all that I had read in Scripture, and all that had transpired, I was forced to consider two options. Either God did not exist, and all that stuff about praying and receiving was goofier than fantasy football, or God was just as the Scriptures said, but my life had moved so far from His truth that I no longer knew how He ran His world. I eventually arrived at the second of those two options: I had strayed from God's ways and had been blinded. But finally, the fog was lifting!

The Holy Spirit showed me scriptures, verse after brilliant verse, that resurrected an understanding of God's truth. Using searchlights like Psalm 66:18, "If I regard iniquity in my heart, the Lord will not hear me," God revealed how I had wandered off His intended path. Another key verse for me was Proverbs 9:10: "The fear of the Lord is the beginning of wisdom." Together, these two verses helped me understand my failure.

First, when we so treasure a sin (we *regard* it) that we ignore God's plan, we undermine the relationship of prayer. Because I treasured my right to set my own rules, I had ignored God and He stopped hearing me—a classic communication breakdown. Second, I learned that people must fear God, not the fear that causes us to hide from God, but the respectful fear that acknowledges God's right to make the rules. Without this fear of God, a person cannot take the first step down the road to wisdom.

As God showed me these basic truths, He also began to wash away Satan's deceptions about my wife. He showed me how my unrealistic expectations of her allowed me to rationalize my lust. My wrong thinking went something like this: "Since Gail doesn't show me love the way I want it, I deserve to check out other women." On one particular day in prayer, God showed me that this attitude was equal to hatred of my wife, the kind of hatred that will

21

hurt others to get its way. I could now see the truths that God showed me because I feared Him—I acknowledged His right to make the rules.

In addition, He gave me the power to obey Him. Now *this* was something new! Before, I may have occasionally wanted to do the right thing, but I couldn't seem to do it, and I certainly couldn't keep at it with any consistency. Now, I had a totally new and effective desire to love my wife as God defines love. "Greater love has no one than this, that one lay down his life for his friends" (John 15:13).

I also saw clearly—painfully clearly—how destructive my unchecked lust would someday be to my children. My behavior horrified me, scared me, and drove me into my Father's arms, crying for mercy and His protection, even protection from my own sinful tendencies. I still cry out for this protection and for His mercy when sinful thoughts cross my mind today. It has been thirty years since Neil was born, and I am grateful to him. In a way, he taught me to pray in the night watches. He turned my heart toward God, and rekindled my marriage. He influenced the souls of his three sisters by making me a godlier husband and parent, which in turn inspired my wife to a stronger relationship with her heavenly Father.

On top of this, Neil made me understand what it felt like to have a son and lose him. I don't compare my loss to that of God, who watched His Son die at the hands of an ungrateful mob. But I do know something of the emotions He felt. If I, sinful as I am, could love a child so much, how much more does God love us? It's a staggering thought, and it takes sixty-six books of the Bible to answer the question.

The pages that follow explore the heart of our Father, and show us how a heart like His creates a strong foundation for parenting.

As someone who has watched a faulty foundation wreck his worldview and almost wreck his marriage, I know how important a foundation can be. The foundation for all things in life, including parenting, is your character, and that's determined by your relationship with God. As you parent, God wants to mold your character right along with your child's. Don't ignore God's work in your own heart as He directs your work on the hearts of your children. By doing so, you can follow Jesus's advice to "first take the log out of your own eye, then you can see clearly to take the speck out of your brother's eye" (Matt. 7:5).

Home Activities for a Good Foundation

1. What are you saying to yourself about your mate? Are you using faulty thinking or expectations to justify your own sinful behavior? "Well, he's not _____, so I'll show him!" Take note of the "inner talk" that goes through your mind as you think about your mate. In 1 Corinthians 11:31, Paul tells us to "Judge yourselves so that you will not be judged." Look hard at your own attitudes to see if you have bitterness that leads you to do mean things, or causes you not to do kind things you know you should. Determine that, no matter what, even if your mate doesn't pull his or her fair share, you will love him or her, putting his or her needs first. If your inner talk about your mate is pure and loving, your actions will follow.

2. Keep a notebook on the spiritual truths you learn through parenting. Your understanding of God is guaranteed to expand as you seek to know His heart as a Father. Keep a list of verses you run across that talk about children in general, and parenting in particular. The book of Proverbs is a particularly rich field to plow.

3. Look at your foundation for life. If you believe in God, does your behavior match your belief? That was my problem. I thought I believed, but my actions did not reflect what I professed. Such a dual personality is destructive. Take a moment and ask God to show you if your actions are consistent with your beliefs. Be prepared for a wild, but joyous, ride as He answers that prayer.

Deception 2:
You're Capable; You Can Do This

Chapter Two
The Lie of Self-Reliance

Maybe it's Satan, or maybe it's just our own pride. Certainly our culture pushes the idea of self-reliance. We all want to think of ourselves as capable of handling the normal expectations of adult life. And parenting is one of those expectations, right? We tell ourselves, "I should be able to raise good kids. How hard can it be? My parents did it. There are thousands of parents all around me, and they seem to get along okay." Satan is the Father of Lies—all of them—and this one is a whopper. Parenting is the toughest of human activities, and God never meant it to be done in self-reliance. *The truth is, you can't do it alone. You need God's wisdom.*

We need to be humble enough to learn about the job of parenting, to ask for help, and to seek the wisdom found in Scripture. God wants us to find and observe good role models. I encountered someone once who desperately needed a role model for her parenting.

Who Is Your Model?

The young girl's heart broke, and suicide was the only fix she could see. While her death was simply a statistic in the local paper the next day, to me it was a personal failure. I had met the girl and her mother exactly once, and only the thirty-something mom spoke that night, while her daughter stewed outside the meeting room. They were new to the area, and the mom was deeply worried about her thirteen-year-old daughter. A divorce had shattered their home and started a series of changes: new town, new school, new home, new church. The daughter was grieving the loss of all that was familiar, but all the mom saw was teenage rebellion. Our discussion was short, but I remember being proud of myself that I had a chance to share some wisdom with that mom. I wasn't proud the next Sunday when I heard the news.

Few details ever surfaced about the suicide. One thing from my brief conversation with the mom pinged around in my memory. She had confided, "I just never had anyone show me how to be a mom." She had come to my seminar asking for advice, but what she desperately needed was a role model.

Who serves as *your* model for the monumental task of parenting? You may not be aware of your parenting model, but you certainly have one. It may be your own parents, or it may be your spouse's parents. Maybe your role model is one of the flawed families on America's TV sitcoms. You may have fallen for Satan's lie that you don't need a good model, that you can figure it out on your own. If you're open to it, I want to suggest a new role model for you. God's model for parenting will help you avoid the deceptions that seek to destroy both you and your children.

The Bible doesn't directly answer questions like "How long should I breastfeed?" or "How should I discipline my three-year-old?" While the Bible does give some direct instruction, it absolutely bursts with over-arching principles related to parenting. Some great books are available that focus on dos and don'ts for parents struggling with particular issues.

Parenting Unchained takes a different approach by pointing you to the ultimate role model. Your model (what you see in your mind as normal and appropriate) is the basis for your attitudes and actions. More than describing parenting techniques that will come and go, this book directs you to the best model for how you live and, subsequently, how you parent.

Raising kids today is tough. Aside from society's moral breakdown, the pace of modern life adds strains unknown in past generations. Yet while the task is tougher than ever, today's parents report for duty less prepared than at any time in the past. In our increasingly mobile society, we are less likely to live near our own parents. Historically, the older generation helped the next generation of moms and dads learn the ropes. Where do parents turn for help today? Wouldn't it be nice if we could see a perfect role model for parenting? Well, God is perfect. What if we could watch Him parent?

While we can't watch God live out a traditional role as parent, the Bible allows us to see God act as a parent in two separate situations: 1) The God of the Old Testament parents the nation of Israel, and 2) Jesus parents a band of followers, His disciples.

Both interactions illustrate how God parented His children—stubborn, disobedient, thickheaded children. Over the course of the Old Testament, God led the nation of Israel from infancy through several phases of growth. In the New Testament, Jesus spent three years preparing twelve disciples for life in a violent, chaotic, and hostile world. In these examples we find the strategies and tactics used by our heavenly Father to prepare His "kids" for the future.

Although Satan prefers that you not look, God reveals Himself clearly in the role of Father. We'll take a close look in the next chapter.

Home Activities to Combat Self-Reliance

1.   The old hymn urged us to 'Count our blessings.' That's not a bad idea for parents as we consider who has helped us along the way. Take a moment to list all the people God has placed in your life to help you: your parents, your aunts, uncles, and grandparents, your church, your teachers, your friends, your enemies who turned out to be important in your growth, the person who led you to faith in Christ, police officers who keep you safe, employers who pay you for the work you do. All of these supporters have contributed to your ability to live and survive on this planet. In light of this list, why do we think we can handle life's challenges alone? As we count these blessings, thank God for them.

2.   We must find the proper mid-point between prideful self-reliance and unhealthy dependence. We all want to take care of ourselves, become independent, and avoid being a burden to others, but in that pursuit we sometimes go too far. The Bible is our best measuring stick for finding that mid-point. It tells us to work hard so we can provide for our needs and those of others (Prov. 13:4 and 2nd Thess. 3:12) but it also tells us to seek counsel (Prov. 13:10) and to assemble together as a church family (Heb. 10:25). The Bible also contains many warnings about pride. We would do well to learn those verses. My favorite, and a good one to teach your children, is Philippians 2:3-4: "Do nothing from selfishness or empty conceit but with humility of mind regard one another as more important than yourselves; do not merely look out for your own personal interests, but also for the interests of others."

Deception 3:
God Only Cares About Rules

Chapter Three
Relationship v. Rules

The most effective lie wraps around a grain of truth. When someone tells an obvious lie, we spot it pretty easily. But when someone starts with the truth and twists it, we get a little confused and don't know where the truth ends and the lie begins.

Many people read the Bible and think it's a book of rules. God is holy, so when He describes Himself, He understandably sets a high standard. And it's true that He wants us to follow His rules so that we will live a healthier and happier life. Thus God's book, the Bible, naturally contains the rules that God knows will help us. But Satan takes these truths and whispers a little twist in our ears.

When Satan spoke to Eve in the garden, he planted a seed of doubt about God's motive. He led Eve to see the beauty of the forbidden fruit without considering God's gracious provision of all the other kinds of fruit she *could* enjoy. Even today, Satan wants us to see God's rules as arbitrary and restrictive. Satan's seduction captures us when we focus on God's limiting rules, yet overlook the truth that *God is a God of relationship*. We bring Satan's false view into our parenting when we focus on the behavior of our children and not on our relationship with them. Let's look at this core truth—it's the most important of all the parenting principles.

Parenting in God's Model Requires a Love Relationship
Our First Proof: God's Self-Portrait

Have you seen God's self-portrait? He created one in the form of a story found in the New Testament book of Luke, chapter 15. Jesus wove a word picture of the Father that was shockingly radical, at least in the view of the religious elite in that day. In this simple story, Jesus painted God as a giving, forgiving, and welcoming Father—absolutely bent on relationship. If Jesus, who is God Himself, gave us such a portrait, surely we should study it in detail to learn what God is like.

Being from Texas, I feel safe in saying that Jesus wanted us to see the Father as a Texan. Well, maybe Jesus didn't *exactly* call God a Texan, but He did paint us a picture of a wealthy rancher, nonetheless. This landowner-father had two sons, each very different from the other. The younger boy was not happy at home, so he rejected Dad and the family business, demanded his share of Daddy's money, and headed out for the fast life. He found it . . . boy, did he ever! In record time he lost his money, his friends, his lovers, and his dignity.

He found himself at the bottom of the job barrel, so he took a "position" tending pigs. In his humiliation, thoroughly defiled, he realized what he had given up back home. Ironically, the runaway had once refused to tend his father's cattle, but here he was, slopping someone else's hogs. He was so hungry the slop looked good enough to eat! He had fallen hard and fast.

But while the boy's journey from pampered son to pamperer of pigs was rapid, the father's wait must have seemed agonizingly long. At least the father had one "good son," the older boy who stayed and worked the ranch. Now, most of us human fathers would take solace in the remaining son and take swipes at the runaway. We might reject the rebel altogether, and we certainly would have a long, hard talk with him if he ever came back. Or perhaps we would put him on "probation," making him prove he had changed for the better before we let down our guard.

But this dad wasn't most dads. He watched the road for his son every day, maybe in expectation, maybe only with a deep piercing pain that wouldn't let him forget.

As the sorrowful son trudged home, he thought, "I'll just live with the hired hands. Maybe I can at least get honest work and eat something decent. No way Dad will want me back after what I did. I hope he let's me get close enough to apologize."

From a distance the father spotted the familiar figure, and what he did next revealed his heart. The old patriarch dropped his dignity and ran toward the son. It was enough for him that the son was returning. Before the son could start his apology, the father "fell on his neck, and kissed him." The boy started in with his rehearsed confession, and he acknowledged he had no right to be called a son.

True, he no longer had a right, but he still had a father who rejoiced to receive him back. The father restored the son from rebellion to righteousness, symbolized by covering the son with the "best robe." Then he placed on the son's hand a ring, symbolizing restoration to proper authority—under the father but over the father's possessions. Finally, Dad put shoes on his son's feet, symbolizing a regained status as heir to the father's wealth and comfort.

All of this bestowed before any discussion of the rules the son would have to accept in order to live in the father's house! Oh, how we need to get this, to see this picture as Jesus painted it! Our love for our children means we care more about the relationship than about the rules. This unconditional love characterizes our heavenly Father, and this same love lays the foundation of a godly approach to parenting. We'll delve into this bottomless well of love in the next chapter.

Before we do, it will be helpful for you to consider your experience with forgiveness from your own childhood. Did your parents make you feel guilty for being a child and making childish mistakes? Did you sense unconditional love from them, or did you sense the need to achieve certain grades, to make the varsity, or to be pretty to earn their love? As you honestly evaluate the plusses and minuses of your upbringing, do you harbor resentment for things your parents did—or didn't do? Maybe a good place to start in your own parenting journey would be to resolve any outstanding hurts from your childhood. I'm not encouraging you to drag up buried hurts and stew on them, but I do encourage you to examine what may be affecting your views on parenting. Understand that your parents were human, and they very likely made mistakes in rearing you. Regardless of whether or not those hurts were resolved to your satisfaction, you can forgive them and choose to look to God as a pattern for perfect parenting.

Chapter Four
If God Isn't Focused on Rules, What *Does* He Want from Us?

Let's continue our discussion of rules. If rules aren't the most important thing to God, what is? As we answer that question, we'll set the stage for parenting in God's model.

Second Proof: God Desired Relationship from the Beginning

My experiences with faulty foundations taught me about God's heart of mercy. As I looked with new eyes through the pages of Scripture, I could see that my experience was consistent with God's eternal way of dealing with all people. From the very beginning, God put relationships before rules, although rules played a part in God's world. Consider a story from the Old Testament book of Genesis, where we get our first recorded view of God as Father. That first view of God will give us a clue to His highest priorities.

As Genesis opens, we learn that God spent several days preparing a place for His climactic creation, Adam. After Adam's creation, God rested, not from exhaustion but to model a lifestyle of periodic rest for Adam. Adam and God communicated daily, walking in the cool of the evening. Adam heard God, and God heard Adam. A world awaited this first caretaker, with all its resources open to the man (and only one thing was off-limits.)

Yet something was missing for Adam. God saw that Adam had no peer and no relationship. Why did God allow Adam to experience this void for a period of time? Why didn't God create both Adam and Eve simultaneously? Perhaps it was to allow Adam to experience and appreciate his primal need for a relationship. The psalmist said it this way: "God sets the solitary in families" (Ps. 68:6 NKJV). God, in His concern to have relationship with humans, made sure His creation would also desire relationship.

Clearly, God desires relationship with us. Otherwise, why would He create humans with the capacity for a relationship? This desire for a love relationship from God toward man radiates throughout Scripture. It rings crystal clear in the Old Testament passage the Jews call the Shema: "Hear, O Israel! The Lord is our God . . . You shall love the Lord your God with all your heart" (Deut. 6:4–5). Christ shone the spotlight of truth on this same Scripture when someone asked Him, "Teacher, which is the great commandment in the Law?" (Matt. 22:36). He, with the sole authority to answer that question, replied, "You shall love the Lord your God with all your heart" (v. 37), and then He added, "You shall love your neighbor as yourself" (v. 39), an Old Testament command from Leviticus 19:18. In fact, Jesus said that all the Old Testament was summed up in these two commandments. God's desire for relationship is pictured and proved best by Christ's death on a cross to reestablish the original closeness between God and Adam. God draws us to Himself through our relationship with Christ. The grand purpose of God for us is a love relationship, first with Him, then with other people.

How can we be sure that God isn't just interested in getting us to behave nicely? How do we know that He desires a relationship with people as flawed as we are? Let's go back to Genesis. It wasn't long after creating man and woman before they dropped the ball and broke that one rule God had set—don't eat from the Tree of the Knowledge of Good and Evil. What did God do in response to Adam and Eve's disobedience? Did He cut His losses and start over with a new man? Did He end the lineage of human-kind and concentrate on the rest of creation? No. He went looking for the man and his wife, calling for them to come out of hiding. In this basic truth—that God comes looking for us—we learn that God cares for us even when we rebel. He could have made man unable to choose wrong, but then true relationship would have been impossible. People can choose evil, and God still comes looking, because God wants a relationship with each individual.

Jump centuries ahead to the book of 2 Chronicles, chapter 30. Here we read that the nation of Israel had wan-dered far away from God . . . again! Hezekiah, a new king, had come to the throne and discovered the long-forgotten book of God's laws. The elaborate rules God gave Moses had slipped from the consciousness of the nation, and all of Israel was out of fellowship with God. The new king had a heart to reestablish the rules, and he determined to celebrate the Passover, the Jews' great commemoration of God's deliverance from Egypt. God's laws required that anyone who wanted to eat the Passover feast should be ceremonially clean, but many of the Israelites could not be ritually cleansed in time for the feast. The king prayed for those whose hearts were in the right place but whose hands were dirty: "May the good Lord pardon everyone who prepares his heart to seek God, the Lord God of his fathers, though not according to the purification rules of the sanctuary" (vv. 18–19). The next verse, verse 20, gives the short and sweet reply: "So the Lord heard Hezekiah and healed the people." In this episode, God heard a prayer and set aside His own rules to heal a sinful people. The rule, though important, gave way to the relationship, which was more important.

So how does a relationship, or lack of it, affect the parenting role? Chip Ingram, president of Walk Thru the Bible ministry, makes a vivid illustration: "Your relationship with your child is a bridge, and your lifestyle values are carried across that bridge to your children. The stronger the bridge, the greater the weight of truth it will hold."[1] God revealed Himself in the Old Testament as a relational God, first with our forefather Adam, then with the nation Israel, from which would come Christ.

Third Proof: Jesus and Relationship

So far we've seen God's self-portrait along with Old Testament proof that God values relationship over rules. Certainly, if Jesus Christ is the expression of God in the New Testament, His work will demonstrate this focus on relationship. Is it possible to find an example of Jesus putting relationship ahead of rules? The problem is not finding an example of Jesus focusing on relationship; the problem is choosing which example out of hundreds! Let's examine one of His last acts on earth.

If ever there were a person more worthless to Jesus than the thief nailed on the cross next to Him, it would be hard to imagine one. We don't know the thief's name, but we do know the Roman justice system had condemned him as a threat to society. You might say he had limitations in his future usefulness to others. In fact, he was moments away from dying. Yet Jesus promised him, "Today you shall be with Me in Paradise" (Luke 23:43). You might be thinking, "Come on, Jesus! This guy doesn't deserve Your mercy. Not only is his past full of darkness, he has no future value to others. How in the world can this thug qualify to be in Your presence eternally?"

I don't understand it, and you can't either. None of us can understand how Jesus wants to spend time with sinners, to redeem us, and even to reward us. None of us deserves His love, and the thief on the cross is full proof that in spite of our abject uselessness, God desires a relationship with us. The thief could not physically obey a single rule after his conversion, attend a single church service, or donate a single dollar, but God still put value on a relationship with that thief more than on one obeyed rule.

Throughout His ministry Jesus placed priority on relationship. Other examples are His meetings with notorious sinners, His call to the tax collectors Matthew and Zaccheus, His mercy on the prostitute dragged before Him, and His rebuke of those who would keep children away from Him.

As parents we must put a relationship with our children even above our justifiable goals for their obedience. Whatever goals we have for our children, if we want to pattern our lives after God, relationship must come first.

In summary, we have these proofs that God puts relationship before rules:
- God created us in His image, and He is relational. He created Adam before Eve so that Adam would recognize his need for relationship.
- Adam and Eve broke the one rule given to them, but God still came for them.
- Jesus proved He cared about relationship over performance by forgiving the thief on the cross.

We should consider one more example before we leave this core truth. Scripture makes the need for relationship clear through the life of a familiar Bible character: King David. But this example shows us what not to do.

Chapter Five
What Happens When the Relationship Is Missing?

Often we learn best by observing the mistakes others make. King David, a man after God's own heart, shows us what happens when the relationship between parent and child is missing.

Fourth Proof: Too Busy to Father

David was a great warrior, a legendary king, and an accomplished songwriter. He had a loving relationship with God. Yet he failed to bring an emphasis on relationship to his role as father to his oldest son, Absalom. Although we're not given details about David's treatment of Absalom as a young child, we can pretty well guess some of the family dynamics in those early years. David was a busy man: first, by running from Saul then running a kingdom. Second, he disobeyed God in that he had more than one wife (not to mention his fling with Bathsheba). Let's see—busy schedule, heavy responsibilities, multiple wives, affair on the side, Uriah's murder to plan, major character flaws to hide—sounds like David might have had some problems giving the necessary attention to his children.

If David's later tendencies are any clue, he shirked his duties as a father. Here's one example from 2nd Samuel, chapter 13: David had multiple wives, and by one of them had a grown son named Amnon. Amnon raped Tamar, David's daughter with a different wife, and the half-sister of Amnon. What did David do in response to this heinous attack under his own roof? David "was angry" but did nothing about this foul deed. Perhaps David found it distasteful to confront his children, but this would prove to be a grave mistake. Developing a parent-child relationship involves loving confrontation over wrongdoing.

Absalom, the brother of Tamar, stewed over this injustice for two years, plotting his revenge against his half-brother Amnon. Where was David during this time? What about the justice that cried out for a father's hand? David was absent, or worse, silent. After Absalom got his revenge by killing the rapist Amnon, David again did a disappearing act, banishing Absalom from the family residence. David chose banishment in order to punish, but he failed to follow it with training to restore righteousness; David simply cut off the already poor relationship he had with Absalom. It was this icy example of relational distance that turned Absalom into a conniving, backstabbing son and a threat to David's kingdom. Absalom became the mortal enemy of David and he would eventually die a tragic death leading a civil war against his father.

In similar ways, parents who shrink from establishing and maintaining relationship with their children may create socially crippled children. While God can heal any hurt or overcome any of the obstacles we put in front of our children, God designed our homes to have an atmosphere of healthy relationship. Ephesians 6:4 tells fathers (and by association mothers as well), "provoke not your children to wrath, but bring them up in the nurture and admonition of the Lord" (KJV). Note that two qualities in the home are required—nurture is listed first, followed by admonition. The order is significant, and it is confirmed by secular research. (See Appendix A for a description of this research and its findings.)

We've looked at the primary truth for parents, that parenting in God's model requires a love relationship. In order to follow God's model we must reject the lie that God only cares about rules. As parents who follow God's model, we must continually check our motives as we interact with our children. We must ask ourselves this question: Do we consciously or unconsciously say "If you obey, I will love you" or do we say "I love you, therefore you need to obey"? It's important to get that order right!

Home Activities for Building Relationships

1. When you spend time with your children, give them your full attention. Don't accept or make phone calls that can wait. When you communicate with them, look them in the eye and make sure they are returning your focus.

2. Engineer times and occasions when your children will talk to you. If your kids are young, you can establish a pattern for this at bedtime, at mealtime, or some other time when the TV is off and your focus is on. If you are still working at the end of the school day, call home when the child arrives home from school and ask about his or her day. Traveling parents can FaceTime or Skype to maintain contact. With older children, especially teens, the time will be harder to structure and maintain, but it is equally critical. With a teen, voice an unpopular opinion on a topic to draw your child out. (With a fifth grader, I might tease an opinion out of them this way: "Drugs and alcohol must make people feel really good, since so many people take them. Why do you think people take drugs?")

Don't get angry when your teenager voices what may seem to be an outrageous opinion. Sometimes they are simply "trying on" different opinions to see which ones fit. You may have to listen at inconvenient times to have any time at all. Give your teen plenty of notice that you want a time to talk. If your teen enjoys a coffee house drink or some other treat, use this as an excuse to get away for some conversation.

3. Be a student of your children—study what they like, and make an effort to become knowledgeable about those

topics. For example, if they like a particular genre of music, learn about a few of the bands in that genre. Then ask your children how some of those bands or artists compare with one another. By asking them a question they can be an authority about, you are giving them a chance to educate you. Make sure that this particular conversation is not about judging them or their music. Those conversations may be necessary at some point, and you must initiate them when you see fit. However, to establish a pattern of conversation with teens, you will need to withhold criticism for the right time and place. Don't badger! Don't keep asking the same question to try to pry information from them. If teens don't respond with a long conversation, that's okay. Badgering will push them away, while a patient approach will be rewarded.

4. Here's an original suggestion (not!): Take family vacations together, and make sure each member of the family suggests some part of the agenda. This doesn't mean that every part of the vacation is designed to cater to your children. I nearly always added an art museum to our vacation agenda, and one of my kids seemed to schedule an ice cream stop somewhere along the way. After years of family vacations, now I'm the one who whines if we don't get ice cream, and my kids have developed an appetite for art museums.

Deception 4:
You Can Be a Parent Without Investing Much Time

Chapter Six
God's Presence

That's a flat-out lie. Parenting is time intensive, and Satan knows it. Why else would he tempt Christians to get so busy with a thousand great opportunities? He knows they will rob us of the time we need to raise godly children. God's example shows us that *parenting is about sharing life with your kids.* There's no substitute for your presence in the life of your child.

You may have heard the story about the little girl who was afraid of the storm. With lightning crackling in the middle of the night, her daddy awoke, not from the thunder, but because of the crying of his little girl. (My wife doesn't believe this story because she knows men can sleep through anything—she thinks it was the girl's mom who got up to comfort her. But it's my book, and I say the dad woke up.) He hurried into her room and took her in his arms. "Don't worry, now. It's just thunder," the father explained, eyes half open. Several minutes passed and the girl was still afraid. "Now, Samantha, you know that God loves us and won't let anything happen to us."

Samantha nodded, but continued crying.

The droopy-eyed dad was dreading the next day—he

needed to get back to bed and get some sleep. "Samantha, listen. Daddy's got to go back to bed. You know you can pray to Jesus, and He'll be right here with you."

"But Daddy, I need a Jesus with skin on!"

We all prefer our love and comfort with *skin on*. That's why there's no substitute for your presence as a parent. Your words, your money, your provision of all of life's physical necessities—none of these is as important for the transmission of your values as the sharing of your life with your child.

Early in the human experience, the physical touch of a parent is key to the infant's proper growth and development. Feeding puts mother and newborn body to body and nourishes the child both physically and emotionally.

In January 1992, I flew to Bucharest, Romania, to install one of the first modern playgrounds in that ravaged country. The Communist tyrant Nicolae Ceausescu had been overthrown just thirteen months earlier, and the bullet holes in many downtown buildings had yet to be patched. What I saw in the orphanage there disturbed me and, at the same time, etched the importance of human touch in my mind. Rows and rows of baby beds contained listless bodies, as if they were products on a shelf. They were methodically fed and clothed yet rarely ever touched. They were literally wasting away. Many had developed severe emotional trauma. Four-year-olds, still in their cribs, looked and acted like two-year-old toddlers, stunted both physically and emotionally. Classic psychology studies from the mid 1900s (Spitz, 1945; Harlow, 1958) demonstrated clearly the essential quality of physical touch for an infant's healthy development.

While Satan tells us that we don't need to spend much

46

time investing in our children, God's treatment of the infant nation of Israel provides a different example. That brings us to another core truth.

God-Modeling Parents Share Life with Their Children
God's Presence with the Infant Nation

In some ways, the birth of the Jewish nation occurred with their deliverance from Egyptian bondage over 3000 years ago. At that time, they became a separate people and were given borders and an identity among the nations. God had protected them in Egypt much the same way a developing child is protected in the womb, a 400-year gestation period! (No wonder Pharaoh was cranky!) During the early days of the exodus, God was visibly and miraculously present with the newborn Israel. "And the Lord was going before them in a pillar of cloud by day to lead them on the way, and in a pillar of fire by night to give them light, that they might travel by day and by night. He did not take away the pillar of cloud by day, nor the pillar of fire by night, from before the people" (Ex. 13:21–22). Note that the Bible says God went in the pillars of cloud and fire. It does not say that God merely *sent* the pillars to guide them. God was present in an extraordinary way within those columns of cloud and fire.

Shortly after this flight from Egypt, God visibly displayed His power on Mount Sinai (see Ex. 19). In fact, God covered the mountain with lightning and smoke while great trumpet blasts rattled the air. The presence of God was so intense the Israelites trembled, begging Moses to hear God on their behalf. Moses spoke comfortingly to the people, "Do not fear, for God has come to test you, and that His fear may be before you, so that you may not sin" (20:20 NKJV).

47

God's presence, though terrifying, was intended to create the proper respect that the children of Israel should show for their heavenly Father, and to help them obey. This is what parents want for their young children—obedience so that they remain safe.

What lessons may we learn from this extraordinary presence of God with the infant Israelite nation? One is that babies need constant care and much direct contact. But even as babies become toddlers and learn to move on their own, eat with their hands, and handle their own routines for hygiene, they still depend on watchful, caring overseers. How did God allow the nation of Israel to learn and grow, yet still provide that watchful care?

God's Presence with Israel in Early Childhood

Israel took its first steps while basking in the glow of God's presence: When God moved, the nation went with Him. When God stayed put, the nation stayed, too. But human toddlers inevitably seek to explore, which often means trouble for parents. How did God channel this energy? God put the young nation to work.

God commanded Israel to build a tabernacle, or tent of meeting, the forerunner of the temple that would be built in Jerusalem. Israel's hands would build it, but it would be done strictly according to the plans God gave them. In Exodus 40:34–38, Moses wrote, "Then the cloud covered the tent of meeting, and the glory of the Lord filled the tabernacle. Moses was not able to enter the tent of meeting, because the cloud had settled on it, and the glory of the Lord filled the tabernacle.. . . For throughout all their journeys, the cloud of the Lord was on the tabernacle by day, and the fire was in it by night, in the sight of all the house of Israel." The Father led the children to do for themselves, to build, and to explore, but He provided a constant overseeing presence and clear guidance.

So must we do with our growing children in the toddler and preschool years—we must give them plenty to do in order to learn. Preschoolers, especially, learn by doing. Tangible, rather than verbal only, lessons work the best.

God commanded the nation of Israel to teach certain truths to its children using tangible lessons, like stone memorials where they crossed the Jordan River, Passover rituals, and feast traditions. Each of these memorials showed spiritual truth through tangible activities. Christian parents should employ similar tools when teaching difficult spiritual or moral truths. You can find great sources for engaging activities in books by Family Time Activities (www.famtime.com) and online through www.d6family/splink.com.

God's Presence with the Child Israel

Somewhere along the way, the pillars of cloud and fire would go away, and I'm sure the nation of Israel wondered why. Just as parents do not spend 100 percent of their time hovering over their children, God removed Himself, in a manner of speaking, by dismissing the pillars of cloud and fire. Of course, God was not gone. Only what was visible to the nation of Israel changed. God had commanded Israel through Moses to make a ceremonial box called the ark of the covenant. In it Moses placed very special items like the stone tablets on which were written the Ten Commandments, a jar of manna, and Aaron's budded staff. God made the ark a symbol of His power and saving mercy. In this new phase, God gave His physical address as the ark of the covenant. "You shall put the mercy seat on top of the ark . . . There I will meet with you; and from above the mercy seat . . . I will speak to you" (Ex. 25:21–22). Of course, God, being spirit (see John 4:24), has no physical resting place, yet God wanted his children to feel a connection to a tangible symbol of His presence, a place of heightened worship and communication. Note, too, that God called the place He would meet them the mercy seat, reminding them of His heart for relationship.

What did God show us about parenting through the addition of the ark and the removal of the pillars of fire and cloud? I believe He leads us to build symbols of important things into our children, so that when we are not in their sight, they will remember and remain true to the relationship. The awe-inspiring sight of fire by night and clouds by day were critical to strengthen and embolden the infant nation. But Israel might never have grown into the next phase of life unless the Father had removed such a commanding presence and become subtler, more inward in the life of the growing nation. We must cease to solve every problem for our children or to dominate their circumstances. We must allow them to exercise skills on their own.

What sorts of things are we to "build" into our children? We must connect them to church, to Bible stories, to songs of the faith by engaging in these activities with them. We must connect them to Jesus as God's greatest expression of Himself, not just telling them about Jesus but also sharing our joy in the relationship. These become the "places" where our children will go to encounter God. Parents take a small step back as we watch our children go to school, Sunday school, or other social settings. Just as God continued to watch his fledgling nation, parents must continue to watch, protect, and monitor the growth of the child. In the early stages of this process, parents cannot just "drop off" their children at church or school. They must experience church and school with their children.

God's Presence with the Young Adult Israel

Many years later, Israel blundered through several periods of rebellion against God. The nation had rejected God's original design to live under Him as their King and, therefore, experienced both victory and defeat. Still, God was present and desired to be more involved. God gave them a great king. David desired to honor his heavenly Father by building a permanent place to worship Him. God allowed David's son Solomon to build the temple. God did not need this permanent building to be present with Israel, nor did He expressly tell David to build Him a temple. In fact, God made Himself present in His words (written by Moses according to God's leading) in the expressions of David's heart and in the wisdom of Solomon. Still it is significant that God allowed the nation to express its desires through a magnificent building program. In the same way, we may not need our grown children to build for us, but we must, like God, allow them to express their own lives and calling without rebuke.

God validated their work when His visual presence filled Solomon's temple on the occasion of its dedication. At this significant time in the life of Israel, God showed His desire to be present by filling the new temple with Himself. "The trumpeters and singers were to make themselves heard with one voice to praise and to glorify the Lord . . . Then the house, the house of the Lord, was filled with a cloud, so that the priests could not stand to minister because of the cloud, for the glory of the Lord filled the house of God" (2 Chron. 5:13-14). God determined always to be available to the nation of Israel in the place and presence of this temple filled with His glory and wisdom. So also should we be available to our children, validating their growing independence by offering our lives and our wisdom whenever they come to us.

Summary

As the nation Israel matured, God remained present through miracles, interventions, and appearances, but these events were never again as visually dominating or as awesome as it was in the infancy of the nation—the exodus from Egypt and the entry into the Promised Land. God changed the nature of His presence to grow and mature the nation of Israel. I believe He planned it this way, and this plan provides guidelines for how we relate to our children.

As we track the growth of the nation of Israel, the changing quality of God's presence establishes the following pattern of good parenting:

- Infancy—Parents are visibly, continuously present.
- Early childhood—Parents are less commanding yet give the child plenty to do to help them learn.
- Childhood—Parents focus on building internal understanding, character, and commitments to the values important to the family.
- Youth and later years—Parents encourage maturity by strategically stepping aside to allow the children to set their own courses.

To follow God's example in rearing children, we must be close at hand in their early years, intervening less and less as our children prepare for life on their own. In the teen years, we must sometimes withdraw (yet watch closely), testing them to see if they are ready for adulthood. In the next chapter we'll see how Jesus's example with the disciples reinforces these same patterns.

Chapter Seven
Jesus: All In, All the Time

As Christ nurtured His band of followers, what was His pattern in this matter of sharing His life with them? I see three remarkable truths in the way Jesus related to His followers.

Truth One: Jesus Was All In

Christians believe that Jesus is not only their Savior but also their God and, as such, was present with God the Father and God the Holy Spirit at creation. Because God desired relationship with human beings, but through Adam all were alienated from God, God sent us His Son, Jesus to reestablish that lost relationship. This is the truth of the verse, John 3:16, "For God so loved the world that He gave His only begotten Son, that whoever believes in Him should not perish, but have eternal life." Jesus, by divesting Himself of heaven to live among humans, illustrated His commitment to being present with us. He chose to spend time as a human in the presence of humans. That's the whole point of God becoming Man: Immanuel—"God with us." And His choice is the same choice we face as we prioritize our lives regarding our children. Will we spend our time in their presence? Not only that, but will we engage with them?

Saying that Jesus prioritized the giving of His time to humankind seems almost the same as saying that Jesus gave a great quantity of time, doesn't it? Not exactly. The difference is subtle but important. Jesus had to decide how to be present before He could decide *how much* to be present. Stated another way, Jesus chose to be fully engaged in the human experience, and that determined the kind of life He lived. He sacrificed much, including heaven and unfettered fellowship with His heavenly Father, to be present with humankind. He chose to experience humanity as a human as a developing child in an economically poor family and in a brutal political climate. He joined us in our fallen state, yet without committing any sin. How does Jesus's example of being all in show us how to parent?

To be like Jesus, parents must be fully engaged in the task of parenting. They must think about and empathize with their children. They must pay attention to their emotional hurts. Parents must remember their own times of frailty and confusion, and thereby respond to children not out of anger but out of compassion and a commitment to train. Just as Jesus did, we must decide to forego some perfectly fine things in order to attain what's best for our children. Occasionally, parents must leave their adult world of privilege to live life with their children—playing hide-and-seek rather than *Call of Duty*. We may have to deny our own needs if we intend to give our children what they need. For example, a father who follows Christ's example will determine that the training of his child must come before his recreational pursuits. Only after making this foundational commitment to be all in can a father make wise, specific decisions about his time and pursuits.

Before having children, I viewed playing in a softball league as a legitimate priority for me. It was my source of exercise and manly fellowship—two good goals. With a new child, old priorities had to move down a notch in my list of things to do. Practically speaking, parents must decide to say no to some otherwise wonderful pursuits to make time available for their children. Once we prioritize parenting at its proper level, only then will our everyday decisions about how to spend our time be appropriate. Our priority—our commitment to train up our children—will thus guard our everyday decisions.

Truth Two: Jesus Gave Quantity Time

Having committed to an all-in engagement, Jesus lavished time on his disciples, allowing them to live in His presence continuously for three years. Jesus took on great responsibility by having disciples. From the onset of Jesus's public ministry, and except for His time in daily prayer with the Father, Jesus spent virtually every minute with His disciples. Jesus didn't have to do it this way. He could have set up a school for disciples, kept them in class for six hours a day, and then sent them home overnight and on weekends. He didn't, and that is a significant parenting model.

In some ways, it is strange to me that the most important person ever to live conducted His public ministry for only three years. The older I get, the shorter three years seem. But in terms of direct instruction, the disciples absolutely feasted on Jesus's time. Scripture gives no hint that the disciples left Jesus's side during their three years of training, except for very brief occasions of Jesus's choosing (when He sent them out on short-term practice missions). They were with Him continuously from the day of their calling to His death on the cross. Then, after three days in the tomb, they saw Him for another forty days. His presence was physical, it was prolonged, it was purposeful, and it was preparatory.

By contrast, the trend in America is for parents to devote less and less time to their children. Our national excuse is that, while we may not spend a large quantity of time with our kids, we will make up for it in quality. Clearly the quantity of time we spend with our kids is dropping precipitously. The *average* worker's commute in my metro area has climbed to more than forty-five minutes each way. In addition, both spouses work outside the home in a growing number of families. George Barna,[2] America's statistician and social trend researcher, estimates "that a century ago parents spent about 54 percent of their waking, married hours in activity related to raising children. Today, the estimate is just 18 percent." Expressed in hours that translates to a drop from 17.28 hours per day to only 5.76 for two parents. Is there enough quality to replace such a drastic loss of quantity? Is the life we give our children today really an upgrade in quality? Little League, soccer, dance, gymnastics, advanced placement courses, and countless other scheduled activities give parents the false sense that they are giving their children every advantage to get ahead. But what kids really need is time with actively engaged parents. And even if we find a way to reverse the trend and spend more time with our children, how do we ensure the quality of that time from a biblical perspective?

One way to guarantee the quality of the time we spend with our children is to follow the mandates of Deuteronomy 6:5–7, which says, "You shall love the Lord your God with all your heart and with all your soul and with all your might. These words, which I am commanding you today, shall be on your heart. You shall teach them diligently to your sons and shall talk of them when you sit in your house and when you walk by the way and when you lie down and when you rise up." First, love the Lord fully yourself. Second, make sure God's Word is on your heart. Third, teach His truths diligently throughout the context of everyday life, not just by taking your children to church!

Let's see how Jesus taught the disciples diligently in the context of everyday life.

Truth Three: Jesus Gave Quality Time

Jesus lived life involving and involved with the disciples. Jesus was called many things, some not so good, but one of the recurring titles given to him was "Rabbi" or Teacher. How did he teach? Did His students attend school during the day and then return home for the evening? No, they followed him, lock, stock, and fishing boat, leaving their former jobs and lives behind.

Luke recounts how Jesus recruited the first disciples. In response to the crowds, Jesus borrowed Peter's boat to use as a stage for speaking. Afterward, Jesus challenged Simon Peter to push back out into the lake, where the previous night's fishing expedition was about as successful as my own dismal fishing trips. Reluctantly, Simon Peter complied, and soon he had to call to other boats to help him haul in the abundant catch, which threatened to swamp two boats. "'Do not fear, from now on you will be catching men.' When they had brought their boats to land, they left everything and followed Him" (Luke 5:10–11). From the beginning, Jesus came to the disciples in their habitats. He involved Himself in the disciples' everyday world.

Jesus had no home during His public ministry; instead, He moved from city to city in Galilee, and His disciples followed him. They went with him to the marriage feast in Cana, to pagan cities like Sidon and Caesarea Philippi, and to the holy city of Jerusalem for the feast days. In short,

His disciples went everywhere He went throughout the region. The disciples learned His habits of early-morning prayer because they were with Him, camping out under the stars on numerous occasions.

Jesus involved the disciples in His ministry, giving them hands-on experience in helping others. They were not simply along for the ride. They handled the finances, arranged logistics, and worked alongside Jesus, ministering to others. Jesus invested in the disciples' lives by teaching, modeling, explaining, equipping, and training. We, too, must look for ways to involve our children in our lives and to get involved in theirs. The secret is to follow God by working as He directs, then to methodically bring our children along in those activities.

Let's flesh this out in one practical way. We each have passions about various aspects of life. Some of you live and breathe sports, and that's not all bad. If you turn your love for sports into an active, healthy lifestyle that involves your children, it's good. If it settles into a whole weekend of ESPN gazing from your perch on the couch, then it's hard to involve your children in that. And simply taking the kids to soccer practice does not truly involve them in an activity of shared presence. Youth sports become simply another spectator sport where your children are the stars and you are the observer. Children sometimes burn out from all the activities, or they resent the pressure parents can put on them. Parents become little more than the source of funds and the bus driver to the sporting event. Instead, find a way to play sports together. This does more to allow you to teach, train, and build relationships. Let your children's talent and inclination in the sport, if any, lead to deeper involvement in team sports. And if your children do become involved in a team sport, be there not just for the development of the sports skill. Look for the ways this activity is developing character. If your children are Christians, see how the fruit of the Spirit is being produced. Ask your children what they are learning about sportsmanship, teamwork, sacrifice, and patience.

The Question of Childcare

How should all these biblical examples instruct us as parents on the issue of who should care for our children? We are not given any prohibition against having others care for our children. Clearly, a principle I see is that children need the presence of a parent, especially early on. There is much debate about the benefits and risks of childcare outside of the home. God's example suggests that young children need the constant presence of a parent. I can't offer you any hard and fast rules, but one Bible story is particularly insightful.

The child Samuel was one of Israel's great leaders in the days before King David. His mother dedicated him to God's service even before he was conceived. She promised God that if He would allow her to have a son, she would dedicate him, even as a child, to God's service. In 1 Samuel 1:24, Hannah took the child to the temple "when she had weaned him," which in Jewish tradition is not before three years of age. Because the child began to serve in the temple right away, I tend to think the "weaning" spoken of here was more likely to be the age at which Samuel was less dependent on others and perhaps able to do simple chores. Thus, I think it more likely that Samuel stayed at home with his mother until at least three, or later. Based on this Bible story, for at least the first three years, children do well to be with a parent, and not in long hours outside the home.

T. Berry Brazelton,[3] a prominent researcher and writer, cautions against non-parental childcare before age three, because many critical accomplishments occur in the first three years of life: sitting up, crawling, walking, talking, potty training, and a thousand other significant "firsts." Parents receive a blessing and children are encouraged when parents get to see and applaud the child as he or she achieves these milestones.

For the parent who has no choice but to use out-of-home caregivers, the rational position would be to 1) delay, if possible, the onset of childcare; 2) limit time in these settings as much as possible; 3) find a setting most like the home; or 4) lean toward in-home care by a grandparent or family friend, if those are safe options.

However, let me be perfectly clear. Good out-of-home childcare is essential to many families.[4] Center-based care, when chosen, works best as a partnership with the parent, meaning that the parent should get to know the staff, become a frequent visitor, and hold the center accountable for the best care possible. Whatever the option chosen for childcare, parents must be sure that the program is both safe and philosophically consistent with their own teachings and values.

Satan has effectively hidden the truth that parenting requires you to be all in. Many parents try to outsource every aspect of parenting: daily care to a childcare center, education to the professional teacher, spiritual training to the church staff. These are valuable resources to parents at various times in life, but parents must reclaim their rightful role as the primary teachers and trainers of their children. God's model shows clearly that He invested His time and presence with His children. He gave His life for us, literally.

Home Activities for Sharing Time Together

1.   Catalog and analyze your interests and passions. Determine which ones can be shared with your children. Some obvious ones are music, sports, reading (which could be extended to observing plays, musicals, or movies), gardening, carpentry, camping, animal husbandry (pets), astronomy, and cooking. As you list your interests, consider how each one might involve your children at their current ages and in the future. Pick one or more that seems to lend itself to involvement of the child. Be prepared to try several activities before you discover which ones spark your child's interest. Make a commitment to invest time in that pursuit *with your child(ren)*. Make sure you focus on the enjoyment of each other's company rather than some product or skill. Finally, look for ways to teach character or teach about God's great provision in these shared times.

2.   For parents who work outside the home, be sure that you regularly discuss with your children what you do at work. Help your spouse, as well as your children, know who you work with, what their prayer needs are, what you struggle with at work, what your joys are, and how God is at work in your workplace. Show your children what you do, and take advantage of programs like Take Your Child to Work day.

3.   Talk to your children as life happens. Ask them what they took away from a sermon, what's happening with any of their friends at school (talking about others is often easier for an adolescent than sharing about themselves), or what they want to do when they grow up. What do they

think about a news report you both just witnessed? Developing the habit of casual conversation and showing genuine interest in their opinions can truly pay off when your children hit their teenage years. If you try to start this habit with your teenage children, be prepared for a long adjustment period. It may take a while to get a silent teen to open up. Hang in there.

4. If you are using childcare outside the home because both you and your spouse work, but you believe that God might want one parent to stay at home, analyze the real costs of keeping that second job.[5] Write the costs and benefits on a piece of paper and find the bottom line. Consider the extra costs for transportation, childcare, illness, wardrobe, and increased income taxes. Consider the added stresses to both parents in child rearing, to both partners in your marriage relationship, and the overall happiness level that the extra income provides. Ultimately, ask God if both parents working is His will for you. No one, including this author, presumes to know what God wants to say to you specifically; however, God gives us the sacred responsibility to raise godly children, and that should make us listen closely to whatever He says on this topic.

Deception 5:
Teaching the Right Information Is Enough

Chapter Eight
Modeling Job

This is the Information Age. We're surrounded by bits and bytes of information. We're so enamored by it, we often think that information is all that matters. As a result, character has taken a backseat. Notice the talking heads at CNN or Fox News. They're always the guys with information—the PhDs, the former executives, the generals. Rarely do they interview the priest, rabbi, or pastor, and even then it's usually a college or seminary professor.

Parents outsource much of their responsibility to schools, coaching clinics, and even churches. One reason is that parents often believe they lack the specialized information needed to train their children, so they defer to others. This plays right into the hands of Satan, who wants us to believe that information is all that's needed to make a good decision. We're told that if we give our kids all the info they need, they'll make good decisions and develop right thinking. But as information has increased and our kids have accelerated their intellectual growth, character training has withered. And our society is paying a price. The Information Age has produced smarter sinners!

God's way is different. While He is the source of all information and is not opposed to science, He desires not just intellectual brilliance but holiness. He calls it wisdom in the book of Proverbs. Consider this verse, "The beginning of wisdom is: Acquire wisdom; And with all your acquiring, get understanding" (Prov. 4:7), and "Hear, my son, and accept my sayings, and the years of your life will be many. I have directed you in the way of wisdom; I have led you in upright paths" (vv. 10–11). God's way is to take information, mix in humility, and turn it into wise living. The writer of this proverb said that he had led his son in right paths. God's way involves leading, and another word for that is modeling.

This brings us to our third core truth, that *modeling is essential to training.*

God Modeled What He Taught

Every parent has had something similar happen, but this might have won the award for "Best Laugh by Congregation at the Expense of a Young Mother." The inexperienced pastor called the children to the front of the packed sanctuary for the Children's Sermon. Dutifully, little boys and girls skipped and skittered from all corners of the room and gathered at his feet. These brief object lessons were always endearing, usually entertaining, and occasionally memorable . . . for the wrong reasons. The pastor, spying an especially stylish little girl dressed in a perfectly pressed and starched dress, fluffed out to attention by several petticoats, asked about her beautiful dress. "That's a beautiful dress you have on, young lady. Is that your favorite dress?"

"Uh-huh, but mommy says it's a b__ch to iron."

Why does your child invariably develop your bad habits, in spite of your efforts to "teach" your child not to acquire them? Do I really have to answer this for you? You know the reason—modeling! Your child copies your behavior, not your lesson plans. Modeling is the most powerful tool in the parent's toolbox, whether you intend to use it or not. Modeling is not an option—it is commanded by God both to use Him as a model and to be a particular kind of model for our children.

In this chapter, we'll see that intentional modeling is what God expects of us as parents. Satan would rather we stop at teaching, but God tells us to include modeling. Let's establish these two commands firmly in our consciousness.

God Commands Us to Follow His Model

We shouldn't be too surprised that God desires for us to use Him as a pattern. After all, the very creation of human beings tells us this in principle. Listen to God's conversation during creation: "God said, 'Let Us make man in Our image, according to Our likeness" (Gen. 1:26). Most evangelical scholars believe that the "Us" here refers to the Trinity; the Father speaks to the Son and the Holy Spirit. Thus God, with the Son and Spirit consenting, determined that humans would be modeled after God. Let that soak in a minute. The Creator of the universe projected His image onto the cosmic wall and drew an outline around it then breathed life into that outline. While we are not God, we bear a resemblance to Him by His own choice.[6]

Having begun in God's image, all people groups and nationalities have an awareness of their specialness in creation. Even non-Christians sense a relationship with a divine Creator, though atheists suppress that inborn sense. All humans, so far removed from that time of creation, are like adopted children who develop a deep urge to locate their birth parents. Men and women throughout the ages and across the continents yearn to find their spiritual Father. As we ponder the creation, our very DNA reminds us of God. Surely, then, if we started in the image of God, we should expect God to desire that we follow in His footsteps.

Whereas this Old Testament passage *implies* that we should follow God's example, the New Testament makes it explicit. Consider these verses:

Matthew 5:48 : "Therefore you are to be perfect, as your heavenly Father is perfect." Jesus makes it clear that our standard of conduct is our Father. Note that Jesus didn't say "your Master" or "your Creator" or even "*the* Father." He said we are to model after *our* Father, reminding us that we possess the genes for the job, if, in fact, we are born of the Spirit.

Philippians 2:5 "Let this mind be in you which was also in Christ Jesus" (NKJV). The apostle Paul commands us to have the same mind-set as Jesus. As He was humble, so must we be. And this brings us to one of the most poignant moments in Jesus's life on earth: Jesus's conversation with His disciples on the last night before the crucifixion.

Jesus, knowing that the Father had given all things into His hands, and that He had come forth from God and was going back to God, got up from supper, and laid aside His garments; and taking a towel, He girded Himself. Then He poured water into the basin and began to wash the disciples' feet and to wipe them with the towel with which He was girded. So He came to Simon Peter. He said to Him, "Lord, do You wash my feet?" Jesus answered and said to him, "What I do you do not realize now, but you will understand hereafter." Peter said to Him, "Never shall You wash my feet!" Jesus answered him, "If I do not wash you, you have no part with Me." . . . So when He had washed their feet and had taken His garments and reclined at the table again, He said to them, "Do you know what I have done to you? You call Me Teacher, and Lord; and you are right, for so I am. If I then, the Lord and the Teacher, washed your feet, you also ought to wash one another's feet. *For I gave you an example, that you also should do as I did to you.* Truly, truly, I say to you, a slave is not greater than his master, nor is one who is sent greater than the one who sent him. If you know these things, you are blessed if you do them." (John 13:3–8, 12–17)

In this sacred moment, Jesus gave us an example and then told us to follow it. I suspect that Jesus's words at the supper might have been forgotten, but His shocking act of servitude was seared upon the minds of the disciples.

God Commands Us to Be a Model for Our Children.

Not only must we follow the example of Christ, we must be an example for our children. This is so obviously woven into Scripture that it is readily assumed but not often overtly stated in the text. God implied this in the command He gave to Adam and Eve, "Be fruitful and multiply." God commands us not just to procreate but to reproduce copies of that original image that God traced on the wall. He says it plainly in Malachi, "Did He not make [husband and wife] one? . . . And why one? He seeks godly offspring" (Mal. 2:15 NKJV). God tells us to raise godly children through a godly example.

God instructed the nation of Israel:

Now this is the commandment, the statutes and the judgments which the Lord your God has commanded

69

me to teach you, *that you might do them* . . . These words, which I am commanding you today, shall be on your heart. You shall teach them diligently to your sons, and shall talk of them when you sit in your house and when you walk by the way and when you lie down, and when you rise up. (Deut. 6:1, 6–7)

First among these words is the command to *do*, not simply to know, what God had taught them. This serves as the proper model. Second, those teachings were to be in their hearts, an internally treasured standard. Finally, they were commanded to teach them to their children in the everyday course of life, at home, on the road, night and day. If I might paraphrase, "Do what's right to teach what's right."

Moving to the New Testament, the apostle Paul commanded his spiritual children to "imitate me, just as I imitate Christ" (1 Cor. 11:1 NKJV). Jesus said to His disciples in Matthew 5:16, "Let your light shine before men in such a way that they may see your good works, and glorify your Father who is in heaven." Whether we have a flashlight or a spotlight, we are to put our good works on display. This is not a command to show off but to let the goodness in you (which is a result of the relationship you have with God) show forth. My first audience is my children, so the command to put our good works on display speaks expressly to me as a parent.

God Shows Us What to Model for Our Children

Okay, so we're convinced that we must model. What must we model? What traits are most crucial for us to model? We have previously discussed the two most important principles God wants to convey to us as His children:

1) relationships trump rules, and 2) God desires to be present in our lives. Consequently, these are the two most important traits to display for our children.

Note that these two traits are intensely personal. You must have a relationship with God, and you must realize that God wants to be present, engaged in your life. If you do not experience these truths, you cannot model them.

In the next few paragraphs, we will review how God modeled them for us. Then, in the next chapter, we'll see how Jesus modeled these two traits, plus a number of others.

Review of the First Two Traits to Model

The foundational principle of parenting is, as we've seen, an emphasis on relationship over rules. God modeled this by sending His Son, Jesus, to die in our place so that He might adopt us into His family. "But as many as received Him, to them He gave the right to become children of God, even to those who believe in His name, who were born, not of blood . . . but of God" (John 1:12-13). This is the essential gospel, that God, knowing we were dead in sin, came to make us alive. Because believers are born of God, we are His children.

If we have a relationship with God, we are invited into His presence. Revelation 3:20 says, "Behold I [Jesus] stand at the door and knock; if anyone hears My voice and opens the door, I will come in to him and will dine with him, and he with Me." This is the offer of the ages; God in Christ speaking to every person. He is knocking, but He won't force His way into our hearts. Jesus not only wants to come into our lives but also to engage in mundane, everyday acts with us, signified by His promise to eat with us.

The most obvious modeling job God did to convey the importance of relationship over rules was to forgive us of our failures. By even once forgiving a sin, God showed us His heart. By forgiving over and over and over and over, God nailed down this principle securely. God loves us in spite of our penchant for breaking His rules. But just because God forgives the sinner doesn't mean He is slack regarding His rules. Jesus took the wrath of God that we all deserved.

God disciplines His children, and His punishment stings, yet God *always* forgives His repentant children. Herein lies the most important instructional guide for us as parents: we must have rules (otherwise forgiveness has no relevance), but we must always convey the truth that rules are the *result* of the relationship, not the cause. Your message must be "I love you, therefore, these are the rules," not "These are the rules. If you obey them, I will love you."

Chapter Nine
God Modeled What He Taught

If teaching information were enough, I suspect Jesus would have been primarily a writer. He could have explained God's heart in books and letters. But Jesus is not the author of any writing that we know of. Jesus taught, sure enough, but it was His modeling that invigorated His words.

How and What Jesus Modeled

Jesus's actions revealed His love for His Father in heaven. He made that relationship public. "Jesus Himself would often slip away to the wilderness and pray" (Luke 5:16), which showed the disciples the importance of a relationship with God. Jesus went regularly to the synagogue, modeling a respect for public worship. Jesus had John baptize Him, modeling obedience to God and submission to men placed in authority.

Jesus Modeled a Desire to Be Present

Jesus modeled His desire to be present with humankind by seeking the presence of sinners: going into the homes of lepers, tax collectors, Pharisees, and even the palace of a pagan governor. He made time for Gentiles, for women, and for children—in other words, for anyone, regardless of their status in society's eyes. When the disciples intended to send the hungry crowds away, Jesus determined to feed them (Matt. 14:15–16). When the disciples wanted to shield Jesus from young children, Jesus took them on His lap and blessed them (19:14).

Thus we see that Jesus modeled clearly how to emphasize relationship, and in so doing revealed His heart to be present with men, women, and children, regardless of position.

In addition, Jesus displayed many character traits belonging to His Father. He modeled

- **broad-mindedness** by talking with people of other ethnic groups, like the Samaritan woman at the well, and by healing the Roman centurion's servant;
- **mercy** by refusing to condemn the adulteress and protecting her from a self-righteous mob;
- **compassion** by responding to the pleas of many for healing;
- **zest for life** by contributing to a wedding celebration;
- **confidence** in the disciples by sending them out on missions;
- **reasoning** by using logical arguments to prove His points;
- **obedience** by returning to Jerusalem in the face of murderous intent; and
- **honor of parents** by providing for his mother, even while He hung on the cross.

The Gospels unearth a mother lode of beautiful virtues to study in our quest to be like Jesus. At the end of chapter 10 you'll find some suggestions for mining Scripture for additional treasures.

Jesus's Model Serves to Equip Us

How do we model godly attitudes and characteristics for our children? Let's examine a point-by-point comparison of how Jesus modeled these characteristics with how we might do so.

How Jesus Modeled Relationship

God forgave; Jesus showed love, respect, and obedience to His Father.

How We Model Relationship

We model a priority for relationship by honoring the person of the child more than the product of the child. In the earliest years, holding, comforting, meeting needs, praising attitudes and accomplishments, and giving eye contact all convey the importance of the person. As children get older, our responses to situations tell them all they need to know about our priorities. For example, when the effort is high on a school assignment but the grade is low, our focus on the grade diminishes the relationship. When she wrecks the car and we worry more about the car than our teenager's emotional health, we demean the person. We also model a priority on relationship when we honor our spouses. If our children sense that their parents' relationship is shaky, they logically may doubt the solidity of their own relationship with Mom or Dad.

How Jesus Modeled Presence

He came down from heaven and lived a completely human life. His ministry model was total immersion, inviting the disciples to live life with Him.

How We Model Presence

There is no substitute for time. If we rarely spend time with our children, no amount of financial support will convince them of their worth. We model a commitment to be present by writing our children's activities on our calendars. We write their school events on the family calendar, and we arrange our time to be there. We may need to do without a new car and larger house so that one parent doesn't have to work outside the home, or we can work fewer hours. Fathers say no to new jobs or added responsibilities so they can commute less and spend more evenings at home. Parents take vacations *with* their kids, not without them. Single parents must make special efforts to maintain their presence.[7]

How Jesus Modeled Mercy

Jesus rejoiced in the restoration of a lost sheep. He praised the sinner who prayed in abject poverty of spirit, and lambasted the self-righteous Pharisee.

How We Model Mercy

When someone hurts you as an adult, pray for that person in front of your children. Help your child to consider the reasons a playmate may be mean, and then pray for that playmate.

How Jesus Modeled Compassion

Christ mourned with the mourner and rejoiced with the partygoer. He met the needs of all who came to Him.

How We Model Compassion

Budget for occasions when a community need arises; then have a family meeting to discuss how much money to donate to that need. Let your children contribute to the fund and welcome their input into the decision-making process.

How Jesus Modeled Zest for Life

Jesus lived the abundant life. He was a man of action,

traveling often and engaging everyone He met. He did not shrink from duty or challenge. Confident of His Father's love, He could enjoy life.

How We Model Zest for Life

Be involved in the world. Meet your neighbors. Enjoy life in front of your children. Laugh. Cry when appropriate. As you participate in activities together as a family, share how God gave you the ability to enjoy that activity.

How Jesus Modeled Broad-mindedness:

Jesus was no respecter of persons. He confronted the rich and powerful when necessary, and he confronted his closest follower, Peter, with his sins. Yet He was tender and caring to the outcasts of His world: the lepers, the poor, the blind, the tax collectors.

How We Model Broad-mindedness

Parents model broad-mindedness by honoring the traditions of other cultures, finding validity even among groups that may be hard to agree with. For example, learning about the expressions of faith in other denominations, even other religions, confirms a respect for others' opinions. Refuse to bash political candidates with opposing views. Speak respectfully of them. This teaches children to respect people we don't agree with. Several simple things you can do as a family will help broaden your perspectives on life, from trying new foods and helping at charities in neighborhoods that aren't like yours to seeing and communicating the good in difficult circumstances.

How Jesus Modeled Confidence

Though He knew His disciples' limitations, Jesus also knew their resources. He gave them jobs to do, including giving His betrayer responsibility for the group's finances.

How We Model Confidence

Expect the best of your children. Let them make as many decisions about their wardrobes, their room arrangements, their methods of doing chores, etc., as their age and ability allow. Model what you want them to do, and limit your corrective language to a small percentage in comparison to your nurturing language. As my longtime business partner taught me, give criticism as a "sandwich": put the critique between two encouraging statements. This forces you to give twice as much positive feedback as negative.

How Jesus Modeled Reasoning

Jesus was a student of the Old Testament Scriptures. He quoted them to fend off temptation and to answer His critics. He took common events and made analogies with them to teach spiritual truths. He turned from the hunted to the hunter when the chief priests challenged the authority by which He taught. He asked them a question, "Was the baptism of John from heaven, or of men?" knowing that any answer would reveal their foolishness (Matt. 21:23–27).

How We Model Reasoning

Encourage your children to think. When they are old enough to pester you with "why" questions, they are old enough to hear your reasons for the rules you set. Avoid telling children to do something just "because I said so." That undermines their view of God as being a God of reason. Model a curiosity about the world. Reinforce that getting an education is the responsibility of every Christian. When tough questions arise, pray with your child, asking God for the answers. Ask your children what they think; then prove you want to know by really listening.

How Jesus Modeled Obedience

Jesus laid aside His reputation, His royalty, and His rights, and willingly suffered indignation.

How We Model Obedience

Obey the law, even the minor ones. Return money when the checkout clerk gives you too much change. Husbands and wives, you have a critical example to set. Wives are to be subject to their husbands, but children should not see this as a bullying husband lording over his wife. The wife should model the right heart attitude in following the leadership of her husband. Grumbling by the wife, even if the husband's lead is followed, conveys that obedience leaves a sour taste in one's mouth. The husband should model obedience by loving his wife as Christ loved the church; sacrificially. Share with your children when God gives you a directive, and be sure to point out the blessings God brings as a result of your obedience.

How Jesus Modeled Honor Toward Parents

Jesus obeyed his parents and likely spent the first twenty-nine years of his life working the family business alongside his earthly father. One of His last acts from the cross was to provide for the care of His mother.

How We Model Honor Toward Parents

Take care of your parents. If you have a poor relationship with a parent, work hard to correct it so it can be a model for the kind of relationship you want to have with your children. Don't speak disrespectfully of your mother or father in front of your children. Make time to call or write your parents, and make sure your children take part in that phone call, or write a paragraph along with your letter. In the same way that you treat your parents, your children will likely treat you. Make a concerted effort to develop a relationship with your in-laws. One of the Bible's most tender and compelling stories is the devotion of Ruth toward her mother-in-law, Naomi. We will prepare our children for a peaceful and successful marriage as we model a loving relationship with in-laws. Sometimes this is difficult, and proper boundaries must be set with parents and in-laws since your marriage partner is now your most significant other. Still, as you honor your parents you create great opportunities to train your children.

Chapter Ten
What If We Don't Practice What We Preach?

To be an effective model, we must add one more key ingredient: our walk must match our talk. Parenting is a no-hypocrisy zone!

A Tale of Two Tools

In college I worked for a construction plumber installing air conditioning units in new apartments. Though I was good in school, it soon became well-known that I struggled to master any mechanical item more complicated than a wheelbarrow. It's not surprising, then, that no one trusted me with the ultimate tool in the construction plumber's toolbox—the two-handed angle drill! (Insert throaty, guttural, manly sounds here.) It weighed at least twenty pounds, and its power was legendary. The angle drill was the ultimate tool, the Hubble Telescope of construction plumbing! We rookies heard whispered stories of the poor guy who just a week before had slipped and gotten his intestines tangled in its spindle. We took turns holding it for the crew boss, and, once, I actually got to press the trigger.

Then the crew boss came to his senses, took away the angle drill, and handed me my assigned tool—the 28-ounce claw hammer. It wasn't motorized, but it could destroy anything! Over the course of that summer, my disappointment turned to respect as I learned how to tear out broken rafters with a single swing and break through roof decking like it was paper. So while the crew boss used the angle drill to construct, I became the designated destroyer.

81

Modeling is a lot like that really powerful angle drill my boss wisely kept away from me. It is the parent's heavy-duty tool for building values into a child. And that 28-ounce hammer is a perfect symbol of the most destructive tool wielded by parents—hypocrisy. It takes a mature, steady hand to model well in front of children, just as it takes a mature and steady hand to operate a large power tool safely. But just as I was able to wreak havoc with that 28-ounce hammer, one swing of hypocrisy can destroy years of teaching.

If you want your children to obey authority, you must model obedience without hypocrisy. Do you obey the rules of the road? Do you speed when there's no police car in sight, then slam on the brakes when you spot a black-and-white car? Even more obvious, do you have a radar detector in your car to avoid getting caught? If so, you're not just modeling bad driving habits, you are modeling disrespect for authority. You are teaching your child to obey when authority is present but to throw off the rules when the authorities aren't looking. No matter how many sermons you preach on obedience, hypocritical actions smash through your ideals like my 28-ounce claw hammer through cheap plywood.

If you want your children to delay gratification so that something better can be gained, like saving an allowance for a major purchase, then you must be able to put off your own whimsical purchases. Dr. David Farmer, a Christian counselor in Fort Worth, Texas, asks attendees at his parenting seminar, "Do your children ever see you say 'No' to yourself?" Many families plunge themselves deeply into debt in order to collect every new gadget, from the latest camera phone to the thinnest LED screen TV. Then they wonder why their children whine to have every new toy marketed on that LED screen.

Even more crucial to the spiritual health of your child is the way parents handle the things of God: is it with or without hypocrisy? If getting to church on time occurs once a month but getting to soccer practice on time is a sacred duty, your child sees the relative priority you put on church. If reading the Bible takes five minutes in your day but reading the sports page takes thirty minutes, your child will weigh the evidence. If your response to the Sunday sermon is a critique of the pastor's presentation and not a discussion of how your life should change, then your child will learn that a church service is entertainment to be judged like last night's reality TV show.

Hypocrisy Damages Children

Children go through a stage of intellectual development during the primary years (ages six to twelve) when their thinking is "concrete." In other words, they see every moral choice as black and white, with very little shading and very little credit given for good intentions. At this age, watching Mom or Dad break a moral code will drastically undermine their respect for their parents. For example, a ten-year-old boy may see his father glance longingly at a scantily clad cheerleader on television. The incident plants deep into the son's psyche a loss of respect for Dad and a diminished value for women. An eight-year-old girl goes through the checkout counter at the store with her mother. Realizing that the attendant gave back more change than was owed, the mother has a choice: speak up and give the money back, or stuff it into her wallet and teach her daughter that ill-gotten gains are okay.

Modeling Is a 24/7/365 Job

Parents don't get to punch a time clock and leave the parenting job at an office. The modeling process goes on as long as your children are awake, and that constancy creates a heavy burden. For this reason, you must guard your quiet time with God so that your spiritual muscles grow strong. Having some time alone is critical for a mother of young children, and all couples need time together, away from their children, to nurture their own relationship. Dirty diapers aren't exactly an aphrodisiac. Organize and plan for opportunities to get away, knowing that in this short season of life, when your children are at home, you're being watched, studied, and copied. The motive is not to get away so you can do those things that are wrong without prying eyes—it's to be at your best when you are with your children.

Satan will tell you that as long as you're saying the right things or taking your children to church to hear them there, you are fulfilling your job as parent. God's example tells us otherwise. Don't dump information on your children. Lead them to consider your wise example as you live an authentic Christian life in front of them.

Home Activities for Character Development

1. Galatians 5:22–23 provides a list of the "fruit of the Spirit." Use this list to search the Gospels for examples of Christ displaying each of these characteristics. Engage older children in this search. Share with younger children your findings. Each fruit could be the subject of a family devotional, including the reading of the gospel scripture, discussion of how Jesus displayed that characteristic, and how we can show evidence of that same fruit at work, school, or home.

2. Play an "I Spy" game looking for those same fruits of the Spirit. Help your children see one of these fruits in action by looking around the house for evidence of a particular fruit. For example, as you go through your house, you may spy a bed made up perfectly. That's an example of a mom's love in action. A piano may remind you of the joy expressed in music. Toys may remind you of how friends play peacefully together. A clock reminds us of patience, and so on.

3. Using a concordance or one of the available online Bible study resources, do a word search for a particular behavior or quality. For example, look for verses that contain both the words *Jesus* and *touched*. Explore the verses and the stories with your children.

4. As a parent, it's hard to know for sure how your children view your behavior. It always helps to ask others if you are achieving your goals. For example, if one of your goals is to be less critical and more positive, ask your children

if your face usually looks happy, sad, mad, scared, etc. If your children are not old enough for this activity, ask your spouse or a peer who will give you an honest answer. Men, it's critical that you give your spouse permission to provide honest feedback on your parenting skills. As a man, I have often been surprised at my own ignorance of my effect on my kids. I'm thankful for a wife who will tell me when my words are too harsh, or when my body language indicates that I'm not listening to my children.

Deception 6:
Why and How You Discipline Don't Matter—Just Make Them Obey

Chapter Eleven
Behavioral Psychology Gone Wild

I fell for this lie big-time. Maybe it's because I considered myself an expert on disciplining kids. After all, I earned a PhD in early childhood education. I knew all the psychological tools for changing behavior. I led seminars on getting kids to obey. I was really good at this in the classroom setting, so I naturally felt I could handle this part of parenting. But success in discipline is more than just getting kids to obey, although the mom in the following story might disagree.

The Mother's Day Massacre

"No, we will not be coming back here anytime soon!" blurted the exasperated mom to her three sobbing children as they opened the minivan doors to head home.

Never, she mumbled to herself, would be too soon. This Mother's Day had not gone the way she had imagined it. That morning her middle child had asked to go out to eat after church at the local children's game-and-pizza place. Taking momentary leave of her senses, and forgetting the enormous leverage she had on this particular holiday, she agreed. She, like her parents, was a staunch teetotaler.

Upon arrival, she was appalled to learn that the pizza place with the extra large rodent roaming around served beer with the pizza. But after twenty minutes of flashing lights, ringing bells, and general chaos, she was ready to order a pitcher herself.

What little confidence she had in her discipline skills had melted away when her youngest darling became the restaurant's center of attention. He had managed to spill two sodas, break up a birthday party, and irritate the giant mouse to the point where Mr. Rodent chased little Johnny up the tube slide and got his giant mouse head stuck in the crawlspace. Dad had been absolutely no help, actually laughing at the whole episode, emboldening Johnny in his display of cruelty to animals. No, they would not be coming back here—ever!

Maybe your discipline skills are under attack the way this mom's were at the Mother's Day Massacre at Rodney Rodent Pizza. Why is it so hard to force your will on the little people living in the room down the hall? Is that even the right goal, to "force your will" on your children? It's so easy as a parent to get off track on this issue. I did.

As I look back on my parenting, my biggest failure was not in my methods, it was in my motives. I'm sad to say that my motives were too often to achieve peace for my own comfort ("You kids be quiet!") or to protect my reputation as a parent ("Be good in front of my friends."). It's not that I did not love my children, it's just that my love for them was not my foremost intention as I chose my discipline times or techniques. I fell for Satan's lie that why and how I disciplined didn't matter, as long as I was getting my kids to obey. But God's truth is revealed as we examine how He disciplined His own. And this brings us to our next core truth: *God disciplined to change the heart, not just behavior.*

God Disciplined His Children To Change Their Hearts

The Right Reason

Over the years I've spoken at dozens of conferences for teachers. Without fail, one topic attracts the biggest crowds: getting kids to behave. Now that I'm teaching parenting seminars, the same priority applies. I can expect strong interest when I advertise a seminar to help parents get their children to obey. Everyone wants to know the how-to of discipline. Parents attend these seminars to learn how to make their children behave.

Until recently, my seminars never addressed the whys of obedience, yet the *reasons* for obedience are more important than the *methods* to achieve it. Christian parents believe that children should obey their parents because the Bible says so. That's true, but is that all parents need to know about the motive? I'd like you to go back to your childhood; retrieve your childhood curiosity and ask the question like a child would: Why? Why should a child obey? Even more to the point, what is our heavenly Father's motivation for teaching us to obey?

Why Is Disciplining Our Children Important to God?

Years ago I would answer this question by saying that God is a God of order, and discipline brings about the order that reflects His nature. Doesn't that sound theologically lofty? Certainly, God is a God of order, and discipline does achieve order among other things, but that's not the primary reason God disciplines His children. He disciplines us (and expects us to discipline our children) because discipline is the way to life, abundant life. Proverbs 6:23 says, "The commandment is a lamp and the teaching is light; and reproofs for discipline are the way of life."

A common theme in Scripture is the benefit of learning from discipline, of hearing God and following Him like a sheep follows a shepherd. Discipline does not presume perfection. In fact, it presumes the need for correction! God knows we will sin and need to be corrected. A wayward sheep will fall into a crag and perish, or wander away from the fold and become easy prey. Sheep need to learn to follow the Shepherd—to accept His discipline and repent when corrected. So the first and primary reason God disciplines us is to provide us with spiritual safety.

The next reason, or perhaps just a deeper expression of the first, is that He loves us. Though I often disciplined my daughters for selfish reasons, I took the time to discipline because I loved them and didn't want them to have a miserable life. Your most basic and enduring reason for disciplining your children is that you love them. Always keep that foremost. Relationship demands that you discipline.

The book of Hebrews in the New Testament shows us God's heart most clearly.

And you have forgotten the exhortation which is addressed to you as sons, "My son, do not regard lightly the discipline of the Lord, nor faint when you are reproved by Him; for those whom the Lord loves He disciplines, and He scourges every son whom He receives." It is for discipline that you endure; God deals with you as with sons; for what son is there whom his father does not discipline? But if you are without discipline, of which all have become partakers, then you are illegitimate children and not sons. Furthermore, we had earthly fathers to discipline us, and we respected them; shall we not much rather be subject to the Father of spirits, and live? For they [earthly fathers] disciplined us for a short time as seemed best to them, but He disciplines us for our good, so that we may share His holiness. (Heb. 12: 5–10)

Pay particular attention to this final statement, because it tells us the ultimate goal of God's discipline. It's always for our good, so that we might share His holiness. Wow, what a great goal! Parents serve God's purpose by rearing godly, holy children (see Malachi 2:15). Part of the parent's job description is providing discipline so that in the end our children will share in the holiness of God. To answer the question "Why is disciplining children important to God?" let's boil it down to this formula: discipline leads to holiness, which leads to life. Jesus said in John 10:10 "I came that they may have life . . ."

Obedience Is Not Enough

To a parent who is struggling to get a child to obey, obedience sounds like a sip of cool water in the desert. But what can look like an oasis can turn out to be a mirage once you arrive. Many parents, including myself, achieved obedience using behavior modification with a child only to find out that they failed to train a more important quality. Two commands in the Bible are directed to children. One does in fact say, "Children, obey your parents in the Lord for this is right." Obedience equals doing what I'm told to do. The other command says something that sounds similar but is significantly more valuable. "Honor your father and your mother." Honor equals doing what I'm told and having a respectful attitude about it. The difference is that a child may obey his parents but not honor them. Honor takes the outward act of obedience and couples it with respect. Obedient children leave home and often may not continue to obey. Children who learn to honor their parents leave home listening to an inner guide who sounds suspiciously like Mother or Father.

Our motive for the discipline we administer is vitally important. If we set out to achieve obedient children because we want to look good in front of our peers, or we simply want to have a peaceful home where chores get done on schedule, then honor is not essential. But if we want to discipline our children to build into them an honoring heart, knowing that this leads to holiness, which in turn leads to life, then our methods will be radically affected.

Will Our Methods Always Work If Our Motives Are Right?

Sadly, no. I wish it were so, but a factor in the equation is easy to forget: your child has to cooperate. The intermediate step, which requires your child to buy in, is for your child to see the benefit of discipline. God desires that your children learn to willingly receive your correction. Thus the greater aim of the discipline of a wise parent is to teach a child to see the benefit of correction. Success in this effort is seen not in the child who always behaves perfectly (this is usually a mirage, anyway) but in the child who accepts discipline with a good attitude and learns from it. Another word for attitude is *heart*. Biblical, lasting discipline focuses on the heart, as Dr. Scott Turansky and Joanne Miller, RN, BSN say throughout their book *Parenting Is Heart Work*.

I focused on behavior, often for the wrong reasons, and because I was so focused on behavior, I did not always see what was happening in my daughters' hearts. God, on the other hand, always sees our hearts clearly and always acts out of a pure motive.

Discover Your Motives

One way to discover our motives is to note what emotions we feel when our children don't obey. Ask yourself, "Do I feel disappointed when my child disobeys?" If so, I may be putting unrealistic expectations on my child. "Do I feel angry when he disobeys?" If so, his disobedience may be a barrier to my personal agenda. "Do I feel embarrassed?" If so, his disobedience may be hurting my reputation with my peer group.

No doubt all these emotions can arise in us, but they should not determine when or how we discipline our children. They may be legitimate signals to say that something is wrong and needs to be addressed. Often the emotion we feel is a legitimate red flag that alerts us to the need to act. At that moment, pray and ask God which discipline tool you should choose to address the disobedience of your child. Sometimes you may need to remove a privilege or apply some other consequence. Sometimes you may need to add training to do the *right* thing. Don't always assume that a negative consequence is needed. "Anger is good for identifying the problem, but not for solving it."[7]

Once we correct our motives, we can think clearly about how to discipline. Life is often so demanding and our lives so busy that we just *do*, without thinking. My parenting was like that, especially as my kids got into middle school and high school. My work, my home life, our kids' activities, and church leadership roles soaked up my planning time for parenting, so I just did what came naturally. I disciplined when I felt like it and for the reasons that just seemed right at the time. But that's not what the Bible tells parents to do, nor is it the model that God provided for parents as He disciplined His children in our two modeling situations. How do we produce in our children a heart that is willing to receive correction? The methods chosen by God with Israel, and by Jesus with His disciples, will give us some ideas. We will look to these methods in the next chapter.

Chapter Twelve
The Particular Ways of Biblical Discipline

Any discussion of discipline techniques, especially in Christian circles, seems to gravitate to the issue of spanking. Some say the Bible demands it. Others say it is a barbaric practice that breeds violent behavior. Neither of these polar opposite positions is particularly helpful to parents, and neither considers the heart of God. If God is our model, we must admit that there were times He used, and still uses, physical means to discipline us, but if we look at the whole of Scripture, we also see God using discussion, instruction, verbal rebukes, laments, and warnings. From the beginning, God reacted to our disobedience by coming for us, talking to us, and making provision for us. God sent prophets, wrote Scripture, and sent His Son to guide His chosen people, His family. This long-range, 30,000-foot view of God's discipline does not lead me first to talk about spanking. So what will we talk about first?

God's Discipline of Israel

As I study God's dealing with Israel, I wonder first how God could be so patient! Virtually from their beginning, the Israelites were stubborn, complaining, and disloyal to God. Yet God never wavered from His plan to put them in the Promised Land. Most scholars put the time of Abraham at 2000 BC, with Moses bringing the nation out of bondage in 1600 BC. The nation reached its zenith in size and prestige with David and Solomon in 1200 BC. And its demise as a free nation occurred with the Babylonian captivity around 580 BC. All through its various phases of birth, growth, maturity, and destruction, the nation of Israel sinned constantly, with only brief exceptions. The sin of the nation grew more consistent and more heinous, and God's warnings became more strident and frequent in the centuries leading to Babylonian captivity. Think of the grand scale of God's patience! He sent prophets, priests, and kings to warn and correct His children over hundreds of years. Surely this speaks of God's patient approach to discipline. His desire was to see His children do the right thing, and His means to accomplish this was patient teaching and correction. Punishment was promised, and it eventually came, but not before God had used every gentle tool He possessed.

When we discuss God's acts of discipline, it is wise to keep His surpassing patience in mind.

Though God was patient with Israel, He did not ignore the nation's misbehavior. Several incidents relate key principles in God's discipline strategies. In the early years of Israel's sojourn, His first strategy was to deliver immediate and tangible consequences.

In Numbers 12, Miriam, Moses and Aaron's sister, questioned the authority of Moses, whom God had appointed leader of the fledgling nation, so God disciplined her with an instant case of leprosy. And you thought sibling rivalry began with your kids! Miriam's sin was pride and rebellion, and God's consequence was painful, immediate, and visible. In the same way, when our children are young, the consequence for rebellion must be painful (strong enough to hurt), immediate (the sooner it is applied, the better the young child connects the wrong behavior with its consequence), and tangible (visible and physical, not just verbal).

In a similar way, God disciplined the Israelite families of Korah, Dathan, and Abiram, opening the earth to swallow them, because they rebelled against God's choice of Aaron as High Priest (Numbers 16). Their discipline was painful, swift, and very visible—to them and the onlookers.

From these examples, I believe it is appropriate to include spanking as one of the viable options for parents of *young* children. This doesn't mean spanking should always be the consequence of choice, but it is condoned, and appropriate for pre-verbal and early verbal children. Taking this example just a bit further, God completely removed Miriam's leprosy, and she suffered no lingering aftereffects. Spanking is not intended to leave scars or brutalize in any way.

Three notes of caution are in order regarding the use of spanking:

1. Don't spank when children get older and their self-esteem may be bruised. A physical blow by a loved one is often experienced as a humiliation and thus creates emotional baggage. There are many better consequence options after age six. After this age, the intellectual ability of the child has grown to the point that verbal rebukes, loss of privileges, or natural consequences can be understood. With my own children, spanking was almost totally ineffective with one of my three daughters by age two, and we were wise to move on to other techniques at an earlier age for her.

2. Painful does not mean harmful. There is a big difference. No spanking should ever leave a bruise or otherwise harm a child.

3. Never spank in anger—it always leaves an emo-

tional red mark. Let me say this again. Never spank in anger. If you are prone to anger, set this particular discipline option to the side. God does not punish His children in anger. He disciplines "for our own good."

A second strategy appears in the way God punished Moses for not following His orders precisely. In Numbers 20:8, God told Moses to speak to the rock in the desert and God would produce water. Moses ignored the instruction of God and struck the rock twice instead of speaking to it. As a result, God removed from Moses the privilege of entering the Promised Land. God confronted Moses with his sin immediately, but the actual loss would not be experienced for some time. I believe this episode gives us some guidance for administering punishment to older children.

First, Moses was generally in harmony with God's will, and he was "mature" and firm in his relationship with God, so his punishment was not physical. God's punishment, though not a physical pain, was a loss of a much-desired privilege, and because it was delayed, was no doubt even more painful to Moses than a prompt bodily punishment. As we discipline older children, we need to confront the problem immediately, but spanking is less effective than the loss of a key privilege—one that the child highly anticipates. I would summarize God's strategy with older children as finding a much-desired privilege then withholding it to teach obedience.

A third strategy is apparent in every disciplinary action of God; each is chosen to achieve a particular purpose. The temporary case of leprosy given to Miriam left no permanent damage but taught both Miriam and the nation the danger of belittling God's leader. The elimination of the family of Korah removed a potential cancer—greed and deception—from the nation of Israel. God's dealing with Moses certainly taught Moses reverence for God's instructions, and it forced the passage of the leadership torch to Joshua at the appropriate time for Israel's journey. In like manner, our choice of disciplinary acts should be made with discretion and to achieve a purpose, not out of reactions like anger or revenge. Waiting until we know what to do serves us, and our children, better than jumping in to correct before we have a clear idea of what we want to achieve. Take time to pray that the discipline tool you choose will teach the precise lesson the child needs to learn.

We need to make one last point regarding God's discipline: it always leaves room for reconciliation. Take for example Peter's boast that he would never abandon Jesus, and Jesus's prediction to the contrary. We are told that immediately after Peter had cursed and denied knowing Christ, his eyes met Christ's. Peter ran away in agonizing shame, yet there was the risen Christ, just a few days later, meeting Peter on the shores of Galilee. In that one-on-one conversation, Jesus asked three times, one for each denial, "Peter, do you love me?" I doubt if I'll ever understand exactly what Jesus was accomplishing, but it seems clear that Jesus was restoring Peter to the ministry and to Himself. After each answer Peter gave that affirmed his love for Jesus, Jesus gave him his charge, "Feed my sheep." As we discipline our children, we must be there on the other side of the punishment, eager to restore, to affirm, and to point them toward their ministries in God's kingdom.

Jesus's Discipline Tactics

In studying Jesus's tactics for training His disciples, we must observe closely the circumstances and methods contained in His teaching. His interaction with the disciples provides fertile ground for a bumper crop of advice. To know what Jesus wants us to do in a given situation requires a thorough knowledge of Scripture and a keen ear to hear the Holy Spirit's instruction.

Jesus Set a Standard of Truth

When Jesus called the disciples, He told them the unadorned truth: they would have to pick up their cross and follow Him (Matt. 16:24); He had no place to lay His head, so His followers were not to expect comfort (8:20); and His followers must give up their rights to choose when to follow (v. 22). In these ways, Jesus made the rules of discipleship clearly known.

For us parents, we must make rules clear to our children. We must speak truth to them, even when the truth is not warm and fuzzy. This is a critical underpinning for successful discipline, as important as the presence of a secure relationship, since children will need to trust you. Anything less than the truth from parents undermines that trust. Hard truth lays a firm foundation.

The truth Jesus taught had a biblical foundation. We need to show the connection between the truth we declare and its biblical origin. Therefore, we must know the Scripture. A wonderful book to keep handy is *Parenting with Scripture* by Kara Durbin. In it the author makes an alphabetized list of key topics you will likely face as parents, for example, selfishness, arguing, and unkindness, and then lists the child-friendly Bible verses that speak to those topics. She includes suggestions to help parents use those verses to teach the positive qualities to children.

Jesus Explained Hard-to-Understand Things

To set a clear standard of behavior, a parent must explain truth clearly and answer hard questions honestly. A mark of Jesus's ministry was His willingness to explain spiritual truth to the sincere questioner. The rich young ruler came to Jesus, asking what he needed to do to be saved, and Jesus gave him more answer than he was willing to hear. The disciples asked Jesus to explain His parables, some of them hard to understand, and Jesus provided clear explanations. John the Baptist, in a moment of wavering faith, sent his followers to ask Jesus the direct question, "Are you the one we have been seeking, or should we look for another?" Jesus answered by reminding John to compare what Jesus was doing with what the Scripture foretold. He did not belittle John for his wanting to confirm such an important truth, and Jesus's answer packed the kind of self-confidence that could withstand a tough question. Jesus even answered the questions and challenges of skeptics. Though many questions were intended to trap Him, Jesus answered even these.

Jesus Nurtured

Fathers are commanded in Ephesians 6:4 to "nurture and admonish" their children. Surely Jesus would live out these same behaviors, and He did. He nurtured and protected His flock by calling them away from the crowds into the wilderness for times of refreshment, by judiciously avoiding Judea when the risk there was great, and by insuring that none of the disciples was taken into custody on the night of His arrest. His encouraging words at the Last Supper were incredibly tender expressions of confidence. Nurturing produced relationship, the tether that would be needed when Jesus had to employ admonition and rebuke.

Jesus Admonished When Necessary

The soft and gentle Jesus is a popular caricature of Christ, but it is far from accurate. He was tough, and we know this not only from the account of His crucifixion, but any logical examination of His life would prove this to us. He lived in a time before any modern conveniences. Everywhere He went, he walked. He grew up poor and labored as a carpenter, probably working with stone as well as wood (since most buildings and public facilities were made of stone in that day). He traveled and lived out in the open, most likely, since He said of Himself, "the Son of Man has nowhere to lay His head." Have you ever seen the skin of a person who lived outdoors most of their lives? No doubt Jesus's skin was rough and leathery, toughened by the arid climate and sun. He was at home among the fishermen of the Sea of Galilee. Such a burly crowd would not have respected him if He had been the soft, pasty-white pansy depicted in medieval paintings.

Similarly, the words of Jesus were often tough and piercing. In one of His sharpest rebukes, He said to Peter, "'Get out of my way, Satan: you are a danger to me because your mind is not on the things of God, but on the things of men.' Then Jesus said to his disciples, 'If any man would come after me, let him give up all, and take up his cross, and come after me'" (Matt. 16:23–24 BBE).

This admonition is even more remarkable because only moments before, Jesus had commended Peter for his spiritual insight. From this we see that a parent must respond to wrong behavior immediately and cannot let evil go unpunished simply because the child usually behaves well. Nor should we punish only when we are in a bad mood and be permissive when we are in a good mood. Our moods should not influence the administration of discipline.

Notice that Jesus bore no grudges. Only a few days later, Jesus took Peter, along with James and John, up on a mountain to witness His transfiguration. While Jesus could rebuke Peter when needed, He did not remove His favor or change the way He treated Peter. Parents must punish on occasion but always in the spirit of persistent love.

Jesus never appeared to rebuke his disciples in anger, but He did admonish with some regularity. Here are some examples:

- Jesus rebuked Peter by asking him where his faith was: "O man of little faith, why were you in doubt?" (Matt. 14:31 BBE)

- Jesus rebuked the disciples when they could not cast a demon out of a boy whose father came to them for help. Then, afterward and in private, Jesus explained why they failed (17:17–21).

- Jesus rebuked the disciples when they attempted to prevent children from coming to Him for blessing. Jesus used the moment to elevate the status of children. "Let the little children come to Me, and do not forbid; for of such is the kingdom of heaven" (19:14 NKJV).

- Jesus rebuked the disciples for criticizing the woman who anointed him with expensive perfume: "Why are you troubling the woman? She has done a kind act to me. For the poor you have ever with you, but me you have not forever" (26:10–11 BBE).

- Jesus rebuked Peter when he boasted about being willing to die for Jesus. The Lord merely predicted the facts of Peter's failure, ". . . before the hour of the cock's cry, you will say three times that you have no knowledge of me" (v. 34 BBE).

In these examples of Christ's admonitions, the causes are particularly instructive. Jesus admonished His disciples for lacking faith, standing in the way of the needy, criticizing a woman's act of worship, and boasting of one's devotion. Jesus did not admonish because of mistakes the disciples made. He admonished them because of wrong heart attitudes: unbelief, insensitivity, a critical spirit, and pride.

Why and how we discipline is of utmost importance, yet obedience is not the final goal for a wise Christian parent. Satan will try to blind you to these truths and tempt you to look only at the yardstick of obedience. Obedience is a good thing, but it ultimately comes out of a changed heart. That's why one of the key goals for parents is to lead their children to a relationship with the One who specializes in heart change. First, ask yourself if you are in right relationship with God; then ask God for wisdom in leading your child to that same relationship. When you ask for His wisdom, your discipline motives and techniques will have God's blessing.

Home Activities Related to Discipline

1. Assess where your children are on the critical heart attributes that matter to God—not just outward behavior but the inner attitudes like humility, respect, sensitivity to the needs of others, and love.

Do this assessment with wisdom, asking God to reveal the truth to you and taking into consideration the opinions of trusted others, like Sunday school teachers, parents of peers and playmates, older couples who have raised godly children, teachers, school counselors, etc. Watch your children in settings where they do not know you are around (observe discreetly). Don't overreact to a single act, but be patient to search out trends of behavior. Don't look just for the misbehavior; look also for the positive signs. In other words, develop an accurate view. Make sure you account for the child's age, since much misbehavior is simply age-appropriate childishness. Be aware of temporary conditions that might affect your child's behavior, like an illness, lack of sleep, or emotionally upsetting events such as a move, death of a grandparent, or divorce.

2. Once you've done a thorough assessment, pick a single important heart attribute to work on. Then develop a set of target behaviors that would indicate progress in that attribute.

For example, if you want to develop sensitivity in your four-year-old son who is not at all sensitive to the needs of others, here are some behaviors you will want to see over time:

- He identifies when a story character is feeling sad, hurt, or angry, etc.

- He acknowledges when a playmate is hurt and shows empathy.
- He says "I'm sorry" when he hurts others accidentally.
- He responds positively to a request to share a toy.
- He sees a need to share and does so without being asked.
- When he sees another child is upset, he takes actions to help.

Now that you've identified some target behaviors, your next step is to sensitize him to the issue. Find stories that introduce characters who are hurt or upset. While reading with your child, ask him about what the characters feel and why. You might connect those characters' feelings to episodes he has experienced ("Do you remember when you didn't get to go to the fair? Do you remember how you felt? I think that's how the bear feels when his friends forgot about him.").

When an upsetting situation occurs during a play session with friends, take the opportunity to point out how the other child feels.

For each target behavior, think of play events or experiences that might elicit the correct behavior. Be watchful to affirm every behavior that gets close to the target. Model and talk about the desired behavior on every appropriate occasion. Note that all these behaviors are not really corrective but are intended to train for appropriate behaviors. Correcting will become important in step-by-step training, but encouraging the right behavior is more important, and should occur more often, than correcting the wrong behavior.

3. And finally, don't read too many parenting books at once. It's easy to get confused and try too many new tactics at one time. Stick to the basics as presented in these three books: *Parenting is Heart Work, Good and Angry,* and *The Christian Parenting Handbook,* all written by Dr. Scott Turansky and Joanne Miller, RN, BSN and available at www.biblicalparenting.org.

Deception 7:
You Don't Need to Talk About Your Faith

Chapter Thirteen
Silence May Not Be Golden

Maybe this lie is the result of a backlash effect. Parents of some religions drill their faith into their kids, and we've all heard stories about Muslim parents disavowing or even harming their children should they leave Islam. We cringe at stories of cult parents brainwashing their children, pulling away from society, dressing in antiquated clothing styles, living in secretive communes, etc. In an effort to avoid this radical approach, many parents go too far the other way and say too little to influence their kids. Words matter, so we need to use them to good purpose. A story I heard about Mark Twain reminds me of this truth in a humorous way.

A renowned politician, famous for blustery and beautiful oratory, came to the city where Samuel Clemens, a.k.a. Mark Twain, lived. Like the rest of the community, Mr. Clemens wanted to hear the great orator, so as a prominent citizen, Clemens was invited to attend. Due to the overflow crowd of dignitaries and community pillars, members of the media were prevented from listening inside the hall, so the reporters waited anxiously outside for Mr. Clemens's comments, expecting to pick up some tidbit of his well-known humor and insight for their various morning papers.

The speech lasted for the scheduled time and then some. An hour passed, an hour and a half, two hours! Finally, the crowd broke from the auditorium, and at long last Clemens appeared, his prominent eyebrows furrowed with obvious frustration. The first reporter to corner him asked him the question on all their minds. "Well, Mr. Clemens, what did he talk about?"

"You know," Clemens cocked his head to consider the question, then paced himself, "he didn't say."

Your Children Need to Hear Your Values and Beliefs

Like the pompous politician, we parents often launch a boatload of words but fail to get our points across. But parents influenced by this particular lie err the other way and say nothing of their faith when their children desperately need to hear teaching on moral issues. Parents have a God-ordained opportunity to teach their key beliefs to their children. While modeling is essential, parents must go further to state convincingly their beliefs. The beliefs your children adopt will one day determine the children's outward actions. Scripture says, "The good man out of the good treasure of his heart brings forth what is good; and the evil man out of the evil treasure brings forth what is evil; for his mouth speaks from that which fills his heart" (Luke 6:45). And Proverbs says, "As [a man] thinks in his heart, so is he" (23:7 NKJV). We are not what we eat but what we think.

What, then, should we put into the hearts and minds of our children? Just as important, what should we endeavor to keep out of our children's minds, and is that a legitimate task given our culture's commitment to freedom of speech? While Satan tells us not to talk about our faith, God says *we must talk about Him diligently to our children.*

We'll begin in a moment to look at what God communicated to Israel, what Jesus taught and how He communicated truth to His disciples. First, we need to plug a hole in the collective head of our culture.

Transferring Your Faith: A Flawed View

I've heard some highly educated parents say, "I don't want to influence my children's religion. I want them to choose for themselves." When I hear this, I know those parents are blinded by Satan and probably have no clue as to what they actually believe. If they really believed anything with certainty, surely they would want to pass that belief on to the children for whom they are responsible. What such a statement reveals about the speaker is this: though they may claim to be Christians, they do not believe in the existence of any absolute truth. Thus it follows that nothing is worth teaching to their children. Taking that point of view, since everyone's truth is unique to him or her, the child's truth is as valid as the parent's. Maybe the child should teach values to the parent!

As ridiculous as this sounds, this reverse education happens in countless homes in our post-modern culture. Parents leave the most critical questions of life (Is there a Creator? Am I responsible to a higher power? What is life's purpose? Do I have an eternal soul? What happens at death?) to their children with very little direct teaching. The ambiguity of the parent toward these fundamental questions leaves a moral vacuum that MTV, CBS, NBC, CNN, and various other cultural outlets rush to fill, so in a sense, our children really are teaching their immature values to an older generation. Here's the question that many parents seem so reluctant to answer: should parents try to instill their foundational views about life, with all their religious implications, in their children?

And the answer is yes, of course! The more pertinent question is *which* views will you instill? As our discussion of modeling made clear, your children will copy what you do, and if your worldview is confusing and unclear even to you, that same confusing and unclear worldview will be lived out before your children. If you believe in a Creator, your children will likely believe the same. If you don't believe there is a God to whom we give an account someday, that view will filter down to your children. If you believe that any path to God will get you there as long as you are sincere, then that idea will very likely come to rest within your children.

Let me give you one example of how your worldview is transmitted to your children through your behavior. Let's say you have just moved to a new city. You look for a church and pick one based not on its members' commitment to a body of truth but because the service always gets out on time, the singing suits your tastes, or the people accept you regardless of your beliefs. You may be communicating to your children that convenience is your greatest value, that style trumps substance, or that any belief is okay as a way to get to God. If you don't go to church at all, you're communicating that God is either non-existent or He is not worth learning about.

You Need to Know What You Believe

Whether you are a Christian parent or not, you must answer a question about Jesus—ignoring the question is an answer, too. Did Jesus tell the truth? I can hear the objections now. "But what we know about Jesus comes from a collection of books that are 2000 years old. How do we know they are really the words of Jesus? Haven't they been misquoted or mistranslated over these 2000 years?" Even among many devout churchgoers, these questions run silent yet deep, eroding and undermining their commitment to orthodox Christianity. If you want to convey a clear belief system to your children, you must be able to state what you believe and why. Often as you rear a child you'll have the opportunity to share your beliefs, but they seem to become more rare as our children reach their teen years. Still, I got such an opportunity driving back from my in-laws' house late one night.

"Daddy, why do you believe in Jesus, Christianity, you know, all that stuff?"

The question came from out of the blue like a spiritual missile. The following are the highlights of what I told my teen daughter:

1. You have to decide for yourself about the key truths of Christianity, and you shouldn't believe what I say just because I say it. You need to think and explore for yourself. (I would be more authoritative to a younger child.)

2. As for me, I believe that the evidence is clear in favor of a Creator. The creation is too complex, and living beings are too complicated to be explained by evolution. The theory of evolution does not satisfy my common sense.

3. If there is a Creator who in some way made the physical world out of nothing, then there is no other miracle that would be too difficult for that Creator. Thus, the Bible's miracles are possible.

4. If there is a Creator and this Creator made me a reasoning, social, and curious being, I believe this Creator made me curious so that I would want to know about Him. Thus, we should have stories of His dealings with men down through the ages.

5. Of all the stories about God (all the religions), only one matches what I see to be true in the world. I see horrible sin committed by people, so I know that sin exists. I see sin in myself, so I know that I am sinful. I see an amazing earth that spins precariously in a hostile vacuum, just the right distance from a heat source so that liquid water is possible, tilted at just the right angle and rotating at just the right speed to limit the temperature range, and with just the right mass to maintain a blanket of atmosphere of just the right mixture to sustain life. Because this world provides so wonderfully for me, I believe the Creator is good. If the Creator is immensely powerful and good but I am sinful, then something went wrong with His creation. The Bible's account of creation and the first man's sin appear true to me. I need a way to be reconciled to my Creator.

6. The way of reconciliation is credibly supplied in Jesus, who is still, after 2000 years, the most captivating and remarkable personality ever to have lived. Because miracles are possible, I am willing to read the New Testament accounts of Jesus and weigh with my intellect whether they are credible. Since the writers of the Gospels do not make themselves out to be superheroes or holier-than-thou figures, these writings ring true. Since the closest followers of Jesus claimed that He rose from the grave, and they

were willing to die horrible deaths rather than recant, I believe they reported exactly what they saw.

7. Based on evidence, I believe that the New Testament books were written soon after Jesus's resurrection, and that they were jealously guarded by the fiercely loyal and heavily persecuted believers of the first few centuries. They were written in Greek, a common language, and there is no controversy today as to what the words mean. Many copies of these books were made early on and even survive today, so that any believer or skeptic down through the centuries could compare and determine if any changes had been made. Many books or letters were excluded from the accepted group of Scriptures, which proves to me that certain rules determined which writings were inspired versus those that were not. Thus, I believe the New Testament is both reliable and inspired.

8. If I believe that Jesus is God and that the New Testament is inspired, then whatever Jesus commands me to do, I have an obligation to do. Because I still drag around an earthly body, I still sin, but I also believe that the infinite value of Christ's death pays for my sin. Thus God, who set up this exchange, accepts that payment in full.

9. Because Jesus spoke of hell and eternal separation from God, I believe in this eventuality for those who reject the offer to believe in Jesus and will not accept His sacrifice.

10. Since I believe in hell, I have a passionate desire to keep my children out of there, and so I take my parenting duties seriously.

I felt pretty proud of myself at the end of my speech. The truth is, I may have used all the right words, but I wish I had spent time listening to her thoughts on the matter. I talked but I didn't communicate. Communication happens only when the words you speak are received as you meant them, and without hearing her thoughts, I couldn't be sure.

By the way, just because you get to have such a conversation with your child, it doesn't mean you've triumphed and the matter is closed. You will have to show that your behavior is based on your core beliefs. You must connect words with actions, as we will consider next.

Connecting Your Words to Action

While much has been said in this book about the value of modeling (walking the walk), there is also a place for reasoning and direct instruction (talking the talk). God made us as reasoning beings, and His great invention within humanity is language. He made us verbal so He could communicate deep truths to us and so we might see that words can create reality, just as He spoke and the world came into being. Thus, God cares deeply what we say, and what our children come to know as a result.

Let me paraphrase a parent's responsibilities this way: We must walk the walk while we talk the walk. Then we must walk the talk so we can talk the talk. Okay, so the paraphrase is actually more confusing. I'll lay it out for you:

- Walk the walk—Parents must *model the desired behavior*.
- Talk the walk—Parents must *provide verbal rules* to explain what they are modeling.
- Walk the talk—Parents must *connect their behavior* to the teaching of Scripture.

- Talk the talk—Parents must be able to *explain why they believe* the Scriptures.

Walking the Walk

We've already discussed the value of modeling those things we want to teach our children, and we've seen Jesus modeling many desirable behaviors for His disciples. But modeling alone can be misunderstood or taken for granted. Thus we must do more than simply provide a silent model.

Talking the Walk

An eighteen-month-old child about to bite a playmate doesn't need a recitation of the rules against hurting others. That child needs Mom's immediate intervention to redirect or prevent the harmful behavior. But even an eighteen-month-old child, after the physical intervention by the adult, needs to hear the verbal rules and the reasons behind the parent's expectations. Though a child might not understand fully her mother's words, those words are connected to accompanying actions each day, and children eventually build their language by these connections. When that eighteen-month-old turns three, the verbalized rules will go with her to a friend's house and serve as an inner guide to her behavior. Of course, her emotions will occasionally overwhelm even the best-taught rules, and discipline may be needed. But little by little, the baby who at one time could only coo and smile will learn one or more complex languages, and be fluent in thinking complex thoughts in those languages.

Please allow me a brief moment to marvel at the gift of language. To me, there is nothing in God's creation more amazing than a child's language development. Think of how we each started—as newborns not knowing who we are or that words even exist. Then consider where we've arrived—as literate readers and writers of a hundred thousand words governed by hundreds of intricate rules of grammar and composition. Most of those rules we can't even enunciate, yet we use them in every oral and written communication. Researchers tell us that the vocabulary of a typical five-year-old is 2500 words. Think about the last five years of your life. Have you learned 2500 new words in that time? Now think about the typical five-year-old. He has been learning those words not from lists or vocabulary-building exercises. He has been learning them strictly from conversations with others, mostly adults. He learned by associating the verbal sounds you make with the things and events flowing in and out of his life moment by moment. Simultaneously, he learned the rules of language along with the vocabulary, again, not by formal teaching, but by logically figuring them out from what you said. He learned what words get an s at the end when they need to be plural. He learned what order the words need to be in to make a sentence. He learned the tenses of verbs, the proper place for me versus my, and hundreds of other language rules. The enormity of the accomplishment is staggering. The miracle of language acquisition causes me to worship God as an amazing Creator! It is no surprise that God, who gave us this glorious gift of language, would speak to us in written language so that His message would be clearly understood.

Walking the Talk

Take every opportunity to live out Scripture in front of your children. When your family must decide a spending issue, involve your children in the process so they can see how you apply biblical wisdom to the task. Share the particular verses you used. When you go through a trial and are tempted to be discouraged, show your children how you draw strength from God's promises and from the fellowship of believers. When you do a good deed, explain how it is being done in obedience to a command of Scripture. When a prayer request is answered, tell your children what you asked and how God answered. Tell your children how God has moved in your life, how He showed you what house to buy, how He got you out of that jam at work, or any of the hundreds of ways God has provided specifically for your needs. In sum, show how the Bible is living and powerful in your life.

Talking the Talk

As your children get older, you'll want to explain why you believe what you believe, just as I did with my daughter. Few people can verbalize why they see the world the way they see it. Most people can't because they fail to consider what their worldview is and where it came from. If you haven't done this, start by writing down what you think about the world, and don't avoid the hard issues. Do you believe in eternal life? Hell? The unqualified goodness of God? The inerrancy of Scripture? The sinfulness of man? As you ask yourself these questions, ask God to show you where your thinking is inconsistent or flawed. I can assure you that if you have not "feared God"—determined that He has a right to direct your life—this exercise will go nowhere. Remember, the fear of the Lord is the beginning of wisdom.

Practice explaining your core beliefs to your spouse or

to a close friend. Read some good books on the subject. Two that I recommend are *The Case for Christ* and *The Case for Faith*, both by Lee Strobel. In these books, Strobel asks the hard questions on our behalf and lets the top experts in the country answer.

The key to talking the talk is taking advantage of little opportunities. Rarely do we get the big question asked directly, as my daughter did on our long car ride. You'll more likely have an issue come up in the ebb and flow of everyday life: going to school, watching a commercial or TV show, or talking about the pastor's sermon. Don't talk down to your children. That's a good way to inhibit their desire to talk with you. As we'll observe in Jesus's conversations, He asked questions, and this tactic honored what the listener brought to the discussion. Ask your children what they think, and affirm their thinking process, even if you need to correct their conclusions.

Chapter Fourteen
God Taught Right and Wrong Through Direct Instruction

Satan wants to shut you up. One way he accomplishes this is by making you feel awkward about verbally sharing your faith with others, even your own children. Satan also has made it a habit to twist and attack God's Words so that we distrust them. That's one way Satan keeps us from studying God's Word. Because we don't fully trust the Bible, we won't invest the time needed to understand it. But God doesn't want ignorant followers. He desires that we study His Word so we can teach it to the next generation. By studying God's Word we learn what God values, what Jesus believed, and how they taught.

God Values His Word.

If God took the time to write what He wanted to say to us, then we know that He expects us to faithfully and accurately pass on those words to our children. Want proof? Here are a few verses to prove that God is serious about His Word.

"You have magnified Your Word according to all Your name" (Ps. 138:2). God would sooner let His name or reputation fail than allow His Word to fail.

"It is written, 'Man shall not live on bread alone, but on every word that proceeds out of the mouth of God'" (Matt. 4:4). Jesus quoted Deuteronomy 8:3 to withstand Satan's temptation to satisfy His physical need. Jesus shows clearly His belief that Scripture is important.

"'This people honors Me with their lips, but their heart

is far away from Me. But in vain do they worship Me, teaching as doctrines the precepts of men.' After Jesus called the crowd to Him, He said to them, 'Hear and understand. It is not what enters into the mouth that defiles a man; but what proceeds out of the mouth, this defiles the man'" (Matt. 15:8–11). Here Jesus makes it clear that simply talking about the Bible's commands, without a heart for actually obeying them is a vain exercise. Christ also sends a warning shot across my bow: "Watch what comes out of your mouth!"

Did Jesus Really Believe the Old Testament?

I hear many religious people endorse the loving Jesus of the New Testament, while rejecting the vindictive God of the Old Testament. Yet much of Jesus's teaching was simply the Old Testament rephrased and illuminated; therefore, Jesus clearly believed the truth of the Old Testament. Jesus often quoted the Old Testament directly. Even as he hung on a cross, he cried out, "My God, my God, why have You forsaken me?" quoting Psalm 22:1. He rebutted Satan by quoting Old Testament Scripture. He taught in a way that reinvigorated truths from the Old Testament: "You have heard that it was said, 'You shall not commit adultery'; but I say to you that everyone who looks at a woman with lust for her has already committed adultery with her in his heart" (Matt. 5:27–28).

Jesus was not one to leave any doubt as to His position, so He said specifically what He thought about Old Testament Scripture, often referred to as "The Law":

> For truly I say to you, until heaven and earth pass away, not the smallest letter or stroke shall pass from the Law until all is accomplished. Whoever then annuls one of

the least of these commandments, and teaches others to do the same, shall be called the least in the kingdom of heaven; but whoever keeps and teaches them, he shall be called great in the kingdom of heaven. (Matt. 5:18–19)

Jesus could not make Himself any clearer about the importance of teaching Old Testament Scripture fully and accurately.

How Did God Teach Values to Israel?

From an overview of the Old Testament, two important patterns of teaching appear. First, God established a relationship before He gave the rules. Second, God's rules were clear, meticulous, and purposeful.

Relationship Before Rules

God spoke directly to the infant nation, leading it by His visible and tangible presence, and providing tangible symbols of His presence through the tabernacle and its contents. God also gave written instructions about all aspects of life in relationship with Him through the first five books of the Old Testament. Later, God gave other books relating the history of His dealings with the nation, providing direction to the worship of the community, offering encouragement and rebuke, and explaining the purpose of the nation in a coming Messiah. The order of these revelations is important for us to see.

The conception of the nation through Abraham occurred first, and God forever referred to Himself as the God of Abraham, Isaac, and Jacob. This name, which He chose for Himself, reminded the nation in years to come of their relationship with God, just as their founding fathers were in covenant relationship to Him. God made that relationship even more poignant by delivering the nation from Egypt and revealing Himself in dramatic ways. Only later, after the birth of the nation and its miraculous extraction from Egypt, did God give the code of rules for His child Israel. The rules came *after* the relationship, yet early in the life of the nation so that it would not be drawn away from that relationship. He gave the written Law (Genesis, Exodus, Leviticus, Numbers, and Deuteronomy) to protect Israel's identity as a unique nation, and to give it a purpose among the nations as a "Light to the Gentiles." In God's larger plan, we know He created Israel for a purpose—to bring the Messiah into the world.

How does this basic truth, that relationship comes before rules, affect us as parents? Simply by reminding us that our rules become necessary as the child grows, but the relationship exists from conception. It also tells us that the rules we create are to serve and strengthen the relationship, not destroy it.

Clear, Meticulous, and Purposeful Rules

The second discernible truth from an overview of the Old Testament is that God's teaching was clear, meticulous, and to a good purpose. The nation of Israel had clear, objective teaching to guide it. The Law was easy to understand and the rules were explicit. For example, the rules governing tithing were specific even to naming the place where the tithes of crops were to be taken, and givers were told what to do if transport was not possible (Deut. 14:22–26). The rules of sexual conduct were clear and precise for each gender (Lev. 18:22 and many more). The rules related to sacrifices were stunningly precise and complete.

In addition, the rules conveyed principles about God's nature. For example, the rule against working on the Sabbath taught the principle that God worked for a period and then rested. If God could rest, then His creation could rest. God's rules for His children created order and equity. Thus, each of Israel's twelve tribes could relax in the knowledge that they were to be treated fairly. Each owner of an animal would know that if his animal wandered away, any finder must return the animal. Each debtor could rest knowing that in the Jubilee year, his family debts would be canceled. Notice that the Law given by Moses to the Israelis was repeated before the nation went into the Promised Land. The name of the Old Testament's fifth book, Deuteronomy, means "second [repeated] law." In this book, Moses reminds and reiterates the heart of God as presented in His Law. We find several lessons for parents from the way God gave Israel rules:

1. Our rules must be clear.
2. They should not be hard to understand.
3. Rules should be repeated often, especially for young children.
4. For young children, rules should be stated positively (do this …) and center on visible, tangible behaviors.
5. As much as possible, rules should be meticulous. (Be gentle. No hitting with your hands or any other part of your body. Walk, don't run, when you are inside somcone's house.)

Our rules should serve a good purpose, not be capricious or simply serve our own selfish needs. For example, requiring a six-year-old child to remain totally quiet for

124

large blocks of time and for no reason ignores the developmental abilities of children. Such a rule will surely cause resentment. However, requiring children to be quiet when Mom is on the telephone teaches respect for others' needs and is tied to a condition that is visible to the child. Because this rule is both reasonable (allows for a manageable time constraint) and tangible (is visible to the child), it is more likely to be obeyed.

How Did Jesus Teach?

As we look to Jesus for a model of teaching strategies, we find at least five observations.

He Taught by Parables and Images

Most of Jesus's teaching employed parables and image-rich language. Jesus taught about God's essential nature through a parable about the prodigal son. Jesus told spiritual truths through parables about farmers, wineskins, grapevines, kings, lenders and debtors, lights and candlesticks, priests and Samaritans. He used agricultural images to explain His mission to an agricultural society: "I am the Good Shepherd" and "Behold, the sower went out to sow." He used relevant imagery to teach His followers their roles: "You are the salt of the earth." Every story drew on what His listeners had experienced and could readily understand.

To imitate Jesus, we need to teach truth at our children's level. The use of parables to teach makes hard concepts easier to grasp. How can we help our children grasp complex concepts? To teach lessons for preschoolers, use tangible and visible materials they can manipulate. To teach a process, make it observable. Imagine trying to teach a three-year-old about God's provision of food. Teaching how wheat becomes bread by planting a wheat seed is not age appropriate because a plant grows so slowly that it is not observable to a child of three. On the other hand, crushing wheat berries to make flour is an observable process and allows the child to participate.

Use word pictures to express difficult or emotionally charged ideas to your older children. For example, I once tried to tell my thirteen-year-old daughter how damaging it would be for her to see a movie with "just a little" bad stuff. Feeling like my words were falling short, I eventually poured a big glass of cola (her favorite drink) over ice and handed it to her. "Hang on a minute though, before you drink it."

As she watched, I went and grabbed an eyedropper from our kitchen drawer, went to the toilet, and drew half a dropper of water from the bowl. "What does this look like?" I asked.

She replied, "Some cold water?"

"Yep, looks like fresh, clean water doesn't it? Actually, though, I got it from the toilet." Then I squirted the water into the glass of Coke. "Okay, now you can drink it."

She hesitated.

"What's wrong? It's just a little bit of toilet water, and the rest of the Coke is just fine."

She got my point—she didn't like it necessarily, but she got it. The inspiration for this tactic came from a wonderful book by Gary Smalley and Jon Trent, *The Language of Love*.[8] In this insightful book, the authors coach you to express your deepest and most significant desires to those you love in a way that gets past their defenses. Jesus did this masterfully well.

Jesus Used Ongoing Events to Teach Important Truths

Although He was eternal, Jesus lived very much "in the moment." He taught by referring to ongoing events. For example, when his disciples were fighting about who would be the big shot in the coming kingdom, Jesus put a little child in the middle of them, and said, "Truly, I say to you, unless you are converted and become like children, you will not enter the kingdom of heaven. Whoever then humbles himself as this child, he is the greatest in the kingdom of heaven. And whoever receives one such child in My name, receives Me" (Matt. 18:3–5).

Near the end of His life on earth, He observed human behavior in the temple. Thousands of people filed through, some making a great show of their generosity. He spotted an event everyone else had overlooked, an old and obviously poor woman making her contribution to God's treasury. "Calling his disciples to Him, He said to them, 'Truly I say to you, this poor widow put in more than all the contributors to the treasury'" (Mark 12:43).

Educators call this technique "seizing the teachable moment." As events occur, as disputes arise, as life is lived, look for the teachings that naturally rise out of those moments. Every positive circumstance is a chance to thank God for His provision. Every negative circumstance is a chance to ask for God's wisdom or deliverance. And in the gathering weight of a thousand little events, the big attitudes of love, trust, and thankfulness are taught. They are not taught in the Sunday school hour, as beneficial as that might be, but on the drive to school, in the line at the grocery store, or during the suggestive commercial at halftime. In these "along the way" moments, parents have their greatest opportunity to share God's truth.

Jesus Explained the Heart Attitudes That Should Accompany the Desired Behavior.

When a Pharisee invited Jesus to his house for dinner, a prostitute, repentant but still possessing her poor reputation, entered the house and poured perfume on Jesus's feet. The wealthy host was baffled that Jesus would allow such a woman to wash His feet with her tears, wipe them with her hair, and, oh my, kiss them with her lips! Knowing the host was indignant, Jesus told a parable of two debtors. One debtor owed a man hundreds of dollars, and the second debtor owed the same man twenty dollars. Both debts were forgiven, and Jesus asked the Pharisee, "So which of them would love him more?" The Pharisee answered, "I suppose the one whom he forgave more" (Luke 7:42–43). Jesus then pointed out that the Pharisee had denied Jesus the customary welcome of a kiss, water to wash His feet, or oil for His dry skin. The woman, to the contrary, had literally poured out her devotion. Through this story, Jesus taught the Pharisee that the one who honored Him was the one who showed love, not the one who proudly adhered to a set of rules.

It was always the heart that mattered to Jesus. Yes, tithe, Jesus said, but don't forget the weightier matters like love and mercy. Of course, do not murder, but also, don't have hatred in your heart. You do well not to commit adultery, but neither should you wish for sex outside of the boundaries set by God.

If we are to imitate Christ in this pattern, we must point out the attitudes that we desire in our children. We cannot be content with outward acts of obedience and inward bitterness, callousness, or rebellion.

There's an oft-told story of the little boy whose dad

made him sit down repeatedly at some stuffy church function. The child's famous reply was "I may be sitting on the outside, but I'm standing up on the inside!" It is precisely this attitude that will require your skillful teaching. Avoid the temptation to force the right words from children without addressing the underlying attitude. Making a child say "I'm sorry" after hitting a sibling is worse than useless unless it is followed up by intentional teaching on repentance, forgiveness, and proper care for others.

It is pointless to try to get children to feel differently than they feel at the moment they misbehave. Emotions flare up quickly, and, fortunately, they also subside quickly. Parents are right to stand by their demands and require the child to be obedient. But later, when the emotion has subsided, share the truth about how God wants us to obey cheerfully, and how an attitude of rebellion disappoints you. Talk with the child about his anger, not to minimize it as invalid, but to talk about how to handle one's anger. Share with the child your own efforts to handle anger. We are no better than our children, just older and better able (hopefully) to deal with strong emotions. Help the child learn to call on God's power to fight wrong impulses, just as you must do.

Jesus Answered Anytime Someone Posed a Sincere Question

Jesus rarely ducked a question. For most of His ministry, He engaged His critics even when their questions were intended to trap Him. Even those powerful politicians who baited Him and sought a way to charge Him with blasphemy received answers. Think of this—even those who sought to murder Him received divine truth. Although they dared to approach their Creator with evil intentions, they were privileged to hear the words of God directly from His mouth. Amazing!

When your children have questions for you, consider it a privilege to answer them. The time will come when they will turn to friends for answers, not to you. Our daughter's hard questions were a daily invitation to get into an argument. She would question the motive of our church in various issues, like why we were building a new education wing when we could be using that money for a mission church. At first, I did not handle these questions as the golden opportunities they were. I would hear only the accusation behind the question and not the mature grappling that was going on in my daughter's heart. While she could have been more respectful in her tone, I could have been wiser in my answers. Over the years, the Holy Spirit within each of us supplied both the respect and the wisdom we each were missing.

He Asked Questions

Jesus asked questions as a strategy for teaching. "Who do people say that the Son of Man is?" (Matt. 16:13). "Why do you call Me 'Lord, Lord,' and do not do what I say?" (Luke 6:46). To the insensitive Pharisees, He asked "Is it lawful to do good or to do harm on the Sabbath, to save a life or to destroy it?" (Luke 6:9).

Psychologists call this teaching strategy "creating cognitive dissonance." In other words, Jesus made His hearers uncomfortable with what they knew or believed—with their convenient but shallow understanding. A good teacher does the same thing with a probing question. "How did that egg get inside the bottle when it is obviously too

130

big to go through this opening?" "Why doesn't the water flow out of the glass when you take it out of the pan upside down?" Solving mysteries of science like these starts with a good question.

Moral mysteries must also be addressed, and your questions can start the process. To a kindergartener, ask, "Why does it always feel bad inside when we get something by taking it away from someone else?" To a fourth grader, ask, "Why do some people lie when they break something?" To a senior in high school, ask, "Why do you think couples who cohabitate before marriage are more likely to divorce than those who live apart before marrying?" In each case, children will grapple with truth to understand it.

Asking questions respects the current knowledge of the hearer and also helps to draw it out. It forces the hearer to become actively engaged in the learning process. It also allows the hearer to come along at his or her own pace. If the question does not produce the desired "dissonance," then the question has no interest for the hearer, and the learning episode ends. If the question produces the desired curiosity, then the learner is motivated to gain new understanding. If I learn something I want to know, it stays with me much longer than something only you want me to know.

So ask your children questions. If they can't answer, or their answers don't satisfy them, then maybe they'll develop an appetite for better answers—answers you can share with them.

Home Activities for Direct Instruction

1. Look at your teaching style. Do you get frustrated if the person you teach doesn't "get it" right away? If so, recognize this as a point of need for yourself and ask God to help you improve your teaching skills. Maybe the problem is that you are a quick study, so you may think everyone should learn at your pace.

2. Study the way your children learn best. Recognize that everyone learns at a different pace, and everyone possesses a unique learning style. Your children might be auditory learners, retaining information better if they hear spoken instruction. They might be visual learners, remembering better those things they can see. Nearly all of us can benefit by having material presented to us in a variety of ways—manually, aurally, and visually. Help your children understand their strengths and weaknesses in learning styles.

3. Observe an expert teacher of your child's age group. Study how that teacher gets information across to children. Ask teachers for tips in working with children the ages of your son(s) or daughter(s). Notice how they gain and hold the attention of the group. Notice what questions they ask and listen for the quality of the responses.

4. Have a family meeting to discuss the rules for your household. Think through the rules that you simply can't negotiate, but invite input from your children on the rules they might want to add. Help your children understand the biblical basis for your house rules. Make sure you include

rules that address proper attitudes. By inviting discussion, you are not abdicating your authority. You have final say in the rules and the consequences.

5. Learn to ask open-ended questions. Instead of asking if your child had a good day at school—which invariably nets a one-syllable reply—try asking about the craziest thing a teacher or student did today. Or ask about their friends' cars, clothes, or opinions. Be sure not to judge their responses.

6. As you watch TV or movies together, you will have the urge to comment on what is wrong about the show or its characters. Be careful to do this in a way that preserves your relationship. Recently, my wife watched a reality show about a polygamist's wives, curious about how these women could interact in such a radically different social environment. I spouted off about its sinfulness and chided her for watching it, without even knowing her motive. I was right in my assessment of polygamy, but I was dead wrong in the way I spoke. I confess, I did this a lot with my children, and it damaged our relationship.

When they were young, we managed their watching habits. As they got older, I wanted to give them room to make some viewing decisions. I would grouse about a show's wickedness, then stomp out of the room in a huff, hoping they would "catch" my point of view and act independently to change the channel. That didn't happen. It would have been better to ask them how the show compared with Bible values and let them come to a biblical conclusion on their own. Take your children through a Bible study that clearly, fully, and graciously helps them see

133

the flaws in the TV show at issue. Ultimately, it's the Word of God that transforms, not our grousing. Go to Summit Ministries (http://www.summit.org) for more information on current media and for tools to develop discernment in this arena.

Deception 8:
Children Should Choose Their Life Course (You Don't Need to Help Them)

Chapter Fifteen
Personal Freedom—The God of This Age

America is all about freedom of choice. Satan has used our idolization of freedom to blind parents to the need to help their children see their purpose in God's plan. While God ordained personal freedom, we ignore the fact that God has given Christians a mission. And if we intend to raise Christian children, we must point them toward that mission. We don't all have the same job to do within the mission. God will lead your children, as He did you, in their specific roles. But the mission itself is clear and applies to all Christians. Second Corinthians 5:18 says that God "reconciled us to Himself through Christ and gave us the ministry of reconciliation." Satan hates clarity of purpose, and he is perfectly happy for Christian parents to remain fuzzy about our mission.

Our model, Jesus, wasn't fuzzy on this point. He diligently prepared His disciples for their mission. This is clear in the ways that Jesus changed His ministry over the three years He spent with the Twelve. Let's study another core truth for parents—*God's children have a mission: Prepare them for it!*

God Helped His Children Find Their Mission
Preparation's Early Steps

Jesus knew when to talk to an individual alone, as He did with Peter, or with small groups, like Peter, James, and John on the Mount of Transfiguration. He knew when an object lesson would work better than a sermon. He also knew what was needed in each step of the development of the disciples.

Like Jesus, we parents must adjust our teaching styles and the key lessons we teach as our children approach adulthood. It helps to develop a "long view," an overall sense of the parenting task. In this chapter, we'll take a step back to develop that long view as we learn through Jesus's preparation of the disciples. We'll look through the lens of Luke, the author of the fourth gospel, to get that long view. Within the flow of stories that Luke shares is a step-by-step progression of Jesus's ministry over a three-year period. We will examine and catalog those stories to find His intentional sequence. From that sequence we'll gather more principles for parenting.

THE BEGINNING OF JESUS'S MINISTRY
TO HIS DISCIPLES

Once Jesus finished His temptations in the Judean badlands (Luke 4), He began His public ministry around the Sea of Galilee. The area of Galilee was a lot like Southern California: a large and diverse population made their homes there. He began to teach in the synagogue of one particular town on the lake, Capernaum; and much like Sundays in America, Jesus went into the home of a local businessman for a meal and fellowship after the worship service. The businessman was named Simon, who would later be called Peter. Trouble was brewing under his tiled roof. Simon's mother-in-law was sick with "a high fever," and the home was in turmoil. According to Luke, Jesus "rebuked the fever" and returned the woman immediately to health.

Jesus continued healing the throngs who sought him out for free medical care, but I'm sure Peter and his wife would be forever impressed by the itinerant preacher from the unremarkable town of Nazareth. Impressed yet uncommitted, Peter went back to work the next day, plying his trade in the local fishing business. But Jesus was not through with Peter. Jesus preached along the shore and the crowd understandably swelled, so much so that Jesus needed a boat to stand in to avoid the press. Guess whose boat just happened to be docked nearby while a certain fisherman washed his nets after a long fish-less night? You guessed it: Peter's. The preacher from Nazareth asked Peter to push out a little from the shore, and using the boat as a pulpit, Jesus taught the crowd while Peter washed and listened there in the shallows of Galilee.

Afterward, Jesus intruded on Peter's turf, telling him to "launch out" into the deeper water and let down the nets, promising a catch. I can imagine Peter's inner conversation: "Who does this preacher think he is? I've been fishing this lake for twenty years, and my father twenty before me. The fish are obviously in some other part of the lake today. This is a waste of time. But . . . he did pray for my mother-in-law, and that was some quick recovery! Maybe I'd better try this, just to humor him."

When the nets came up bursting with fish, Peter hollered for his partners to bring a second boat, and it, too, filled to the brink. The ships were in danger of capsizing from their load!

Suddenly Peter realized the miracle that was happening around him, and he fell down at Jesus's knees. "Go away from me Lord, for I am a sinful man!" Jesus reassured Peter and challenged him, all at the same time, saying, "Do not fear, from now on you will be catching men" (Luke 5:8,10).

In these two episodes, Jesus met the personal need of Peter then called him into a relationship and a mission. In the same way, a parent's work involves two phases: 1) establishing a relationship by serving; then 2) preparing their children to serve. In the long view of parenting, we must clearly see the end purpose for which we have been given our children. They are on loan to us from God, meant to come into a relationship with Him and meant to go on a mission—a fishing expedition, actually—catching other people for God's kingdom.

Before we go on to other stories in Luke's gospel, let's be sure we see the practical aspect of Peter's enlistment. Jesus unselfishly entered Peter's life, giving to his family, and meeting the immediate needs in Peter's life. Only afterward did Jesus move Peter toward a deeper commitment, calling him into a ministry partnership. With our children, we will spend years simply giving and giving and giving, but little by little we will encourage them to become partners with us in God's grand plan of service to others. If we give and give yet fail to prepare our children to serve others, we will have unleashed on the world spoiled brats. If we fail to build relationship and instead only prepare our children for a job, though they be noble jobs, we will unleash on the world needy, unloved, and unloving workers, missing the joy and the self-esteem that would make others want to follow them.

CALLED TO PROTECT OUR CHILDREN

All good parents will go to great lengths to protect their children from threats of physical harm. In fact, the nearest I came to a real beating from my saintly mother was when she thought I was going to run into the street to retrieve a baseball. I'm not sure which would have caused more pain, old man Crawford's 1961 Chevy Impala, or the switch my mom pulled off our Chinese elm tree. Baseball announcers talk about the tremendous bat speed generated by today's major league hitters. Ha! My mom could make a switch whistle like a teapot. In that episode, a mother's fear for the safety of her little one produced appropriate boundaries and speedy consequences. But today, many parents fail to set boundaries on the visual temptations, R-rated movies, video games, and popular music that are piped into our living rooms and mobile devices daily. I'm amazed at how many of our Christian friends allow their children to watch movies that even a secular entertainment industry warns about. It's no longer uncommon for second graders to know enough about the sex act to engage in mock intercourse at school. They may be unclear about all the details, but they aren't blind! They see the bare-shouldered couples humping and huffing in a bedroom scene, and they know from the faces that something good's going on. Yet many parents either knowingly allow such shows to be seen, or are sadly unaware of the number of such episodes that their children will see on prime-time TV or in PG and PG-13 movies. Where are the protective walls that in former years kept our children from developing an inappropriate appetite for sensuality? Gone, or in severe disrepair, I'm afraid.

Jesus gave us a proper example by protecting His disciples, especially early in their training. In Luke chapter 5, Jesus's band of disciples came under the criticism of the legalists of the day. The scribes and Pharisees complained against His disciples saying, "Why do you eat and drink with the tax collectors and sinners?" They also complained "The disciples of John often fast and offer prayers, the disciples of the Pharisees also do the same, but Yours eat and drink" (vv. 30, 33). To both complaints Jesus spoke up for his band of followers. He answered directly to these critics and did not leave the disciples to defend themselves. In this sense, Jesus sheltered His disciples from the criticism of the world around them. On several occasions, Jesus took the disciples away from the crowds to rest and to learn. In one of Jesus's last acts, He commanded the soldiers who captured Him in the garden of Gethsemane to let His disciples go free. They did.

Parents, too, must provide shelter for their children. Clearly, in the preschool and early elementary school years, no amount of protection from harmful ideas and social pressures is out of line. Movies and TV viewing should be limited to only those that are consistent with Christian ethics and values. If evil is depicted in a movie or TV show seen by a child, the parent should speak immediately with the child about what he or she saw. Extreme violence and vivid, scary images will usually result in night fears among young children. As children enter the upper elementary years, their ability to process make-believe images like TV and movies becomes such that rational discussion can help them deal with those images. Explaining the destructiveness of the behavior to the child, why it is inconsistent with Scripture, why people act that way, and how they should have acted all are important steps successful parents take to help their children process difficult and frightening thoughts.

CALLED TO PRIORITIZE OUR RELATIONSHIP

Next, Jesus went out to pray alone on the mountain all night (Luke 6:12). When he came down, he gathered the large group of followers and then selected a group of twelve He called apostles, which means "sent out ones." Jesus thus began the process of enlisting disciples to join in an intentional, eternal ministry. He was looking toward the day when those disciples would carry on in His absence, just as our children will do one day. Jesus would continue to teach the large crowds who followed Him, but He measured His resources of companionship and closeness, investing heavily in this small band of "children." We parents are duty-bound to limit our investment, our relationships, to our own children so we can accomplish our family's purpose. This may mean limiting our community-volunteer efforts, or perhaps even putting on hold our climb up the corporate ladder, so that we have sufficient resources to devote to our children.

Later in Luke 10:41, Jesus made this point clear when he told Martha, who was focused on her duties as hostess and homeowner, that she was "worried and bothered about so many things; but only one thing is necessary." Martha's sister, Mary, by contrast, was soaking up the words and relationship Jesus presented. When pressed to choose between duties to the world and the opportunity to grow the parent-child relationship, we, like Mary, should choose the relationship.

A very short but telling episode in Jesus's life even

reminds us to guard our role as parents against improper intrusion by our families of origin. Jesus's mother, brothers, and sisters came to where he was teaching, seeking time with Him.

> And His mother and His brothers came to Him. And they were unable to get to Him because of the crowd. And it was reported to Him, "Your mother and Your brothers are standing outside, wishing to see You." But He answered and said to them, "My mother and My brothers are these who hear the Word of God and do it." (Luke 8:19–21)

In this same situation, I would be tempted to drop what I was doing and devote time to my original family. Yet Jesus did not do so. He used the moment to emphasize His mission, the importance of a relationship to God through hearing His Word, and doing it. The relationship with God is more important than an adult's relationship to parents and siblings.

At times, we parents are tempted to put our parenting mission on hold, to defer to our parents in critical matters such as discipline or core beliefs. If we are to follow Jesus's leading, we must not allow even grandparents to assume our parenting responsibilities. Nothing, not even our children's grandparents, should come between us and our duty to rear godly children.

We are responsible for the experience our children have around their grandparents. If that experience is not beneficial, if grandparents go overboard indulging our children, or if they refuse to maintain the rules we believe are necessary for our children, parents must draw boundaries of behavior for grandparents. This is not to say that grandparents and other family members should be ignored or cut off, only that their proper role is to support you in raising the children God gave you. Pray for grace-filled words to explain this responsibility to grandparents.

CALLED TO PREPARE OUR CHILDREN

Immediately after this episode, Jesus entered a boat to cross the lake to another region where the Jewish influence was subdued. The journey itself hints at a new direction in Jesus's ministry and in the preparation of the twelve apostles.

What are the marks of this preparation? One is the purposeful move toward a more hostile region. The disciples would see in this move Jesus's love for people outside the Jewish culture. Another is the backing away from moment-by-moment protection of the disciples. We see this when Jesus napped on the boat. While Jesus slept, a storm swept over the lake. The disciples frantically sought to wake Jesus. On awakening, He "rebuked the wind," and the sea became calm. I believe Jesus was giving the disciples a chance to grow up, to show an independent faith in God. The disciples may have failed in this instance, but the event was a necessary step in preparing for "adulthood."

In the same way, we must create opportunities for our children to experience storms while we are nearby. We can watch to see how our children respond, and we must not be discouraged when the lesson must be repeated. This same lesson on the Sea of Galilee would be repeated numerous times, and Jesus gave the Twelve other similar tests.

Let's think practically about the implications of this point. How do we back away from the moment-by-moment protection of our children, and when? An obvious way we do this is by sending our children into a school setting. While some parents are properly convicted to homeschool their children, this can be taken to an unproductive extreme. The desire to shelter children from evil is admirable, but it should not be used to avoid preparing children for life outside the home. Homeschooling parents will need to find ways to safely place their children in situations that encourage self-reliance. I know many homeschool parents who do prepare their children for the harsh realities of the real world, yet some shelter to the point of inhibiting growth.

Parents must be fully involved with their children's education. I believe God leads some parents to public schools, and He leads others to private schools or to homeschooling. Regardless of school setting, children must go through a progression of reduced parental oversight. This progression might come through extracurricular experiences like organized sports or music lessons, Sunday school, summer camps, etc. Parents' prime responsibility is to arrange experiences that will be both safe and challenging for their children, away from the parents' direct supervision more often as children reach maturity.

Jesus set up tests for His disciples as we'll see in the next chapter. Sometimes they passed, and sometimes they failed miserably. But He was there to console, encourage, and send them out again.

Chapter Sixteen
Preparing For Service

One of the paradoxes of Christian life is that the surest path to personal freedom is through submission to Christ. Jesus said this Himself when He told His Jewish audience '"Truly, truly, I say to you, everyone who commits sin is the slave of sin. . . So if the Son makes you free, you will be free indeed" (John 8:34, 36). This sort of freedom only comes when we submit to Christ—serve Him, becoming the servant of others as He commands. It's not natural for us as adults to put our own interests aside and serve others, and it's certainly not natural for our kids. But that's Christ's will for them. Satan's desire is for children to throw off all parental guidance. Unbelievably, parents comply when they fall for the lie that they have no right to tell their children what their mission is. Christian parents have that right, but it takes intense preparation.

The Preparation Intensifies
Later Steps

Next in the book of Luke, we see that Jesus quickened the pace of His disciples' preparation, giving them "practice" for the mission ahead. Chapter 9 tells us that Jesus gathered the Twelve and "gave them power and authority" and then sent the disciples out to preach and minister in the local community. Jesus gave them instructions for this practice period and sent them on their way. We parents can learn some lessons from this.

First, this practice did not occur until after the previous preparations and testing had been accomplished. Don't send your children out into the world until you've had plenty of time to teach them at your side, exposing them to good work habits, building a foundation of a strong relationship with you, and teaching them about God's love for them.

Second, give children what they will need to accomplish their life's task. Jesus gave the Twelve "power and authority." Most parents will spend eighteen years building abilities and talents into their children. We will teach children to read, to write, to develop their talents, and to experience the world. They will need social skills to survive and thrive in their jobs. They will need an understanding of money and commerce. This all may seem self-evident, but some parents fail to help their children see that true stewardship requires doing one's best at school and in developing character, so that we can give back to God our best efforts. Clearly, many parents put pressure on children to perform, but they fail to teach them the proper reason for doing their best. It isn't to get ahead or solely to please the parent but to give glory to God by serving others well.

Third, create opportunities for "practice" ministry close to home. Jesus could have sent the disciples to a foreign country, as He did at the end of His earthly ministry through the Great Commission. But this practice ministry was in the towns around the region of Galilee. Why did Jesus limit the range of ministry? It's not explicitly stated, but some apparent reasons are that the practice event could be a short, limited time. Jesus could gather them back together and get their feedback, seeing what they had learned and what they still needed to learn. By starting close to home, the twelve disciples ministered in familiar territory to more sympathetic listeners. This helped to make these initial efforts successful. Early service or mission experiences we set up for our children should also be positive.

Fourth, challenge your children with increasingly independent opportunities to minister. The first and most obvious place of ministry is at home to the family. Next is the local church. Your child should grow up, literally and figuratively, in a local congregation of believers. Raising children within a healthy church family helps prepare them for service. Youth ministries that take groups of teens on mission trips provide tremendous benefit, and some of that benefit is because the parent stays home. (This is not a substitute for families serving together.) Teens learn to develop a heart for ministry that is not thrust on them by their parents. Such independent ministry opportunities allow God to build a direct relationship with your child. In the same way that the disciples were told not to take money with them, your teens will go without your direct protection and resources, forcing them to rely on God's provision from sources other than yours.

Fifth, follow up. Share in the joy of ministry by your children. When the disciples returned from their time of ministry, they told Jesus all that they had done. In one account (Luke 10:17–20), they all rejoiced in the miracles that God worked through them, and Jesus used that joy to teach about God's heart.

In this account, the disciples returned with new vigor, rejoicing with each other that even the demons obeyed them. Jesus reminded them to rejoice not in their dominion over demons but in the fact that "your names are written in heaven." Jesus pointed the disciples to the unsurpassed value of a relationship with God, worth far more than flashy displays of the miraculous.

Use every success of your children to give praise to God. As you do, you teach your children that their ultimate service is to Him, not to you as parent. You also build their self-esteem based on the only lasting reason in this world: that God loves them and has a plan for them.

CALLED TO CHALLENGE OUR CHILDREN'S FAITH

Immediately after the success of their practice ministry, Jesus was deluged by the multitudes. At the end of the day, the twelve disciples were worn out and wanted to send the crowd away to find food and lodging, since the place where Jesus taught was out in the country. But Jesus told His disciples, "You give them something to eat," not "*Let's do this*" but "You do it!" Their response? The Twelve, with eyes limited to the current lack of food, reported only what they could see at hand—five loaves and two fish.

Remember that just prior to this, these same disciples had been given power and authority to heal the sick and cast out demons. They had watched Jesus perform amazing miracles. Yet in the face of this new need, they had no faith for this task. Is it possible that Jesus really meant for the disciples to work a miracle? From His directive "You give them something to eat," I believe so. But when they failed in this, Jesus still found a purpose for them. He instructed them to organize the crowd into groups of fifty, then after blessing the bread and the fish, Jesus enlisted the disciples to pass out the miraculous increase.

Jesus gave His disciples an opportunity to stretch their faith, but when they failed, He did not cast them aside. He engaged them in work they were able to do and made them partners in His ministry. We must do the same for our children. Give them authority and abilities, then challenge

148

them to use their gifts in ways that require a stretch. If they accept the challenge, great, but even if they don't, we must involve them in ways that match their abilities.

CALLED TO CHALLENGE OUR CHILDREN'S VIEW OF CHRIST

"Who do the people say that I am?" Jesus asked. The rumors flew around Galilee and the whole region, including present-day Israel, Lebanon, Jordan, and Syria. Some claimed that Jesus was John the Baptist come back from the dead; others believed that Elijah walked among them. The disciples tossed out a host of other prophets' names. But Jesus pressed them personally, "Who do you say that I am?" The disciples would not be able to hide behind the rumors and the private opinions that dodged personal accountability. Jesus wanted to know how each one of them answered. This was a question with eternal implications.

The disciples had seen Jesus do things no man had ever done. They had heard him speak about Scripture with an authority that could come from only the author. Jesus had forgiven sins, walked on water, raised a dead child to life, and as they watched He had turned five loaves into food for 5,000. But still, to call someone who was so human, so average, so familiar . . . Messiah, God of Israel? Now that required going out on a limb. Who else but bodacious Peter would speak first? "You are the Christ, the Son of the living God" (Matt. 16:16). The Christ, the Son, the living God. Where did Peter get such an unbelievable idea? Not from human sources, according to Jesus. In Matthew's account of this conversation, Jesus responded that such information was revealed by "My Father who is in heaven" (v. 17).

Sooner or later, we must determine what our children

believe about Jesus. "Who do you say that I am?" is an important question, and parents must ask it of their children. But parents can only provide the facts about salvation to the child. God must reveal the truth of Jesus's claim to be God and the Redeemer of humankind. As parents we must remember our role and our limits. It is not enough for our children to know what others, including parents, say about Jesus. They must decide for themselves, and God Himself must prompt such faith. I find it interesting that Jesus gave the disciples proof of His nature, but even Jesus did not make them believe. That is the unseen work of the Holy Spirit, and while we can plant the seed of truth in our children and provide an environment conducive to growth, the germination of that seed is not up to us.

Certainly by the teen years, parents should expect their children to develop their own convictions. To avoid spiritual questions is to leave such important matters to chance. From my point of view, it is far healthier for a child to have honest doubts about God and Jesus and to feel confident enough to ask their parents tough questions than for them to pretend to believe. I would rather know what my child is thinking, even if it is a challenge to my own faith, than to wrongly assume my child is a believer. Invite your children to express their doubts. The very confidence you show in listening sympathetically to these doubts will serve as proof of the existence of God and His redeeming work in your life. Admit your own doubts and share how God is helping you deal with them.

TEACHINGS OF JESUS IN THE LAST HALF OF HIS MINISTRY

With Peter's great confession now out in the open, the

disciples knew clearly who Jesus claimed to be. He would spend the next months sharing more directly about His own plans, and preparing the disciples for life after the cross. From Peter's confession to the time of Jesus's arrest in the garden of Gethsemane on the night before His death (Luke 9:21—22:46), Luke reported sixty-eight separate events or parables in Jesus's life. Each event or teaching episode shows a concerted effort to prepare the disciples for life as independent believers, to convince the rest of the world of the truth about Himself, and to prepare the disciples for opposition by unbelievers. Along the way, He continued to heal and work miracles even as He shifted to a more earnest phase of teaching. Confrontations with the power structure of His day grew more common and more vehement. My own review of these sixty-eight events leads me to certain conclusions about how Jesus prepared the disciples, and suggests six emphases that parents should consider as they prepare their maturing children for life after leaving home. (See Appendix A for a listing of these sixty-eight events.)

1. Based strictly on the number of teaching events, Jesus's highest teaching priority in this phase centered on the cost of discipleship. Those who chose to follow Him were expected to take up their crosses, to be courageous in the face of opposition, to maintain their focus on the task at hand, to persist when the battle continues long, and to avoid the traps of wealth or earthly passions, which might derail their missions. Seventeen of the sixty-eight events dealt specifically with the costs of discipleship.

2. Next in Jesus's priority of lessons was His relentless insistence on pure character and motives: to

be humble, thankful, and devoted. On more than one occasion, Jesus taught His disciples to have an attitude of a little child: expectant, humble, and grateful. When a Samaritan community rejected the disciples, He corrected those disciples who would have called down fire on the town. Jesus reminded them that His mission was one of redemption not retribution. These events accounted for fifteen of the sixty-eight teaching episodes.

3. Next, Jesus taught explicitly about persisting in prayer and preparing for the time when He would leave them. Prayer would be the disciples' lifeline to God the Father through the person of Christ by the help of the Holy Spirit. Additional teachings in this category prepared the disciples for the spiritual battles to come. These teachings numbered ten of the sixty-eight.

4. Jesus told parables or engaged in events that revealed who He was and what the Father was like. One event was the Transfiguration, where Peter, James, and John saw Jesus in His glorified state. These lessons about His divinity also numbered ten of sixty-eight.

5. Jesus warned both the disciples and unbelievers about hell, the destruction of Jerusalem, the damage done by particular sins (like cheap and unnecessary divorce), and the failure of any person to repent and turn to God. I counted nine such warning lessons among the sixty-eight.

6. Finally, Jesus confronted His enemies on seven occasions in this section of Luke's gospel. On each occasion except one, Jesus answered the charges of

His attackers, offering them the truth that would set them free, though their questions were booby traps meant to rob Jesus of His freedom.

From this examination, I see several important points. First, Jesus made sure His children knew the responsibilities that came with being part of a family. That cost would involve sacrifice, courage, focus, and learning to avoid the snares of petty pleasures. In fact, I believe the second most common topic of His lessons, an insistence on pure character and motives, is really just an extension of these responsibilities of being an heir of Jesus. Combining these two groups of events makes for a startling realization. Jesus was most concerned that His children learn what it meant to be one of His heirs—their responsibilities to be a particular type of person, with high character and pure motives.

We can follow Jesus's example by continuing to teach our children throughout their teen years to concentrate on character. We can remind them of their mission as a child of God, a member of a church family, and a member of a unique earthly family.

But what does it mean to be a member of your family? What is your family's mission? You can't explain what you don't understand, and you can't pass on what you don't have, so you must take time to develop your family mission statement. At the end of this chapter are some family mission-building activities. These will help you examine your purposes and passions. Some will help children become aware of and supportive of the family's mission. Other activities are designed to encourage children to think of their own life purposes.

Jesus taught His disciples to expect persecution, and He

was frank about the consequences of rejecting salvation. As our children get older, we should not hide from them the pain of the world. Those with televisions in our homes can hardly avoid large doses of the world's reality. Newspaper headlines and the evening news present plenty of opportunities to talk openly with teenagers about sin and its consequences. We have a sacred duty to be truthful about humankind's fallen nature. For example, teenage girls need to hear that a man's lust is difficult to tame and destructive in many ways.

Luke's gospel shows a clear progression as Jesus parents His twelve disciples. It begins with acts of protection and service. It ends with some reality-based preparation for a tough world.

Parents can fall for Satan's lie and let their children flounder as they search for their mission in life, or they can follow the example of Jesus. In the next chapter, we'll look at the final adjustments Jesus made as He prepared His disciples for independent, mature life in the world. Satan would prefer that parents make no adjustments, and that's the basis for his next deception.

Home Activities for Family Mission Building

1. Donate a day of work at a local food kitchen, adopt a family for the holiday season, visit residents in a local rest home or hospital, or help a widow with chores. After your day of service, talk with your family about how the project went, what they felt, and how God spoke to them. Get opinions on whether a particular project should be repeated. This analysis will help your family zero in on a particular direction of ministry.

2. Take a family mission trip. The age of your children will determine the type of trip and the location. Younger children may need to stay with a grandparent. When children are preschool age, the best ministry will be within the family or neighborhood, so they can see the immediate impact in an understandable setting. Taking food to neighbors is a great start, and your children can learn some cooking skills at the same time. The following ministries exist with the express purpose of helping families become mission minded:

    Family Legacy Missions International:
    www.legacymissions.org
    Adventures in Missions:
    www.adventures.org

3. Discuss your family's resources around the dinner table, and ask family members why God has given your family these particular resources. Include each member's talents and desires. Especially, don't forget each person's apparent faults that God might use for good. Help your children see that one's weaknesses today can be the very thing God uses tomorrow.

4. Ask each member of your family (teens and older) what their "soft spot" is. Your soft spot is the issue or people group that evokes in you a desire to minister to that group. My soft spot is parents heading toward divorce, families in trouble, and children in need. For some, their soft spot is the lost people of a particular ethnic group or those in financial bondage or the elderly. A wise Christian leader pointed out to me that the recurring tug of the Holy Spirit on my heart was a sign of the particular need God created me to fill. Once those soft spots are identified, find concrete ways for each family member to make a difference in that issue or people group.

5. Write out your family's mission statement. After doing the four previous mission-building activities, you may know more about how God has created your family and your collective mission. Once you've written your mission statement, you might even see your job as a parent more clearly.

Deception 9:
It's All About Consistency (You Don't Need to Adapt)

Chapter Seventeen

A Good Quality Overused

O ne of the mantras of behavioral psychology is the need to be consistent in your parenting. Satan takes this principle and deceives parents into over-using it. While consistency in daily schedules and in applying rules helps with young children, parents can take this too far. They feel like they have to maintain a steady course, even when that course is not working, so they resist change to the detriment of their parenting. God's example shows us that *parents must adapt as their children mature.*

The truth is that children are complex and they change rapidly. Things that worked yesterday may not work today. One of the biggest mistakes parents make is to doggedly maintain the control they had when their children were young, even as children hit the teen years. Control sounds like a good idea, but it can backfire in parenting and in governments as well. Consider the surprising story of neighboring kingdoms.

The Parable of the Two Kingdoms

Two kings sat on thrones of neighboring countries. Each was a good king, but the king of the eastern king-

157

dom excelled in most ways above the king of the west. If the western king had 100 chariots, the eastern king had 200. In the matter of castles, the eastern king built a more splendid one. His entourage was greater, his tax base larger, his conquests more memorable than the king of the west. The fame of the eastern king far exceeded that of the good but unremarkable king of the west.

It came to pass that each king grew old and died. The great eastern king had held tightly to his power until the very end, seeing that no one could govern as well as he had. The western king was not so impressive in his accomplishments, however, and had been forced to share power as he got older, to the extent that he had given to one or the other of his sons, and even to several top administrators within the kingdom, most of his authority.

Kings from far away came to the funerals of both kings, as they each had died within only a week of the other. Even in death, the eastern king had impressed the other emperors with a grand state funeral full of pomp and circumstance. The sadness of the citizens seemed to prove how much the eastern king would be missed, as the citizens of the east were far more downcast than those of the west.

Yet the years that followed showed an odd sort of disparity between the exalted eastern kingdom and its lesser western neighbor.

The western kingdom continued its modest prosperity and even began to gain esteem on the international stage, its economy bustling and its leaders proving their capabilities with every crisis and opportunity. The eastern kingdom, sorely missing its beloved king, declined sharply as the new and untested leaders fought among themselves for preeminence and control of the country. Decisions made by one governor were reversed or undermined by another, and the hole left by the great eastern king grew more obvious and more cankerous by the month. Citizens fled from the eastern to the western kingdom when war broke out between the competing factions. The once strong eastern economy oozed away like the blood of the citizens drafted to fight their vicious civil war.

How did such a turnabout occur? How could the mighty kingdom of the east slip so far so fast? The answers lie in the nearsighted policies of the greater king, who through consistent control failed to prepare his kingdom for his departure. Tragically, I see many parents who make a similar mistake, overvaluing consistency with respect to control. They fail to make key adjustments that prepare their children for the time when they will make decisions outside of the parents' control or influence. Valedictorians and football stars alike go away to college, full of dreams, only to make a royal mess of life. This should not be so.

How can parents adjust to better prepare their kids for life away from home? What steps can parents take to smooth the transition in the high school years to prepare for launch? To heck with "smooth," how can I improve the chances that my children won't go wild and self-destruct when they leave the protection of my home?

We turn again to the ultimate source of wisdom, the example of Christ, who marked the final stage of preparation of His disciples with three key adjustments: an increased emphasis on prayer, an introduction to the Holy Spirit, and a move from the tutoring relationship toward friendship. All three of these shifts model a change of relationship between parent and child, and each offers important guidance for parents.

Jesus Emphasized Prayer—Communication with God

Near the end of His time on earth, Jesus said, "These things I did not say to you in the beginning, because I was with you. But now I am going to Him who sent Me" (John 16:4–5). Jesus knew His time on earth was nearing an end, so He had to introduce a new way to communicate. He had to teach His disciples about prayer. As Jesus approached the end of His time on earth, He modeled and taught on this topic with increasing urgency.

All four Gospels present Jesus's considerable body of teaching on prayer. Luke 11 records several parables on prayer plus Jesus's model prayer, which we refer to as the Lord's Prayer. In Luke 18, Jesus spoke parables on the importance of persistent prayer, and contrasted a proud church leader's prayer with a humble sinner's prayer. These teachings, placed in the later chapters of Luke, reveal that Jesus increased His focus on prayer as a key preparation for the disciples' lives after Jesus's ascension. But the clearest evidence of this emphasis on prayer is seen in the last several chapters in John's gospel.

Beginning with chapter 13, John recorded Jesus's last moments with His disciples. Jesus knew the hour of His death rapidly approached, thus He focused on those teachings that were desperately critical to the next phase of life for the disciples. Look at the following list of verses and their content:

"Whatever you ask in My name, that will I do, so that the Father may be glorified in the Son" (John 14: 13–14). Several points are made here about prayer: 1) Asking is based on our relationship ("ask in My name"); 2) our asking makes a difference ("that I will do"); and 3) God gets the glory from this communication and relationship ("that the Father may be glorified"). Parents must take communication with their children seriously. Jesus did.

"If you abide in Me and My words abide in you, ask whatever you wish and it will be done for you" (15:7). Jesus's words and their residence in us determine the success of our prayers!

"Truly, truly, I say to you, if you ask the Father for anything in My name, He will give it to you. Until now you have asked for nothing in My name; ask; and you will receive, so that your joy may be made full" (16:23–24). Jesus told them directly that a new arrangement, different from the past one, was just around the corner ("until now"). He also promised that this new relationship of communication would bring a fullness of joy.

"In that day you will ask in My name, and I do not say to you that I will request of the Father on your behalf; for the Father Himself loves you, because you have loved Me . . . I am leaving the world again and going to the Father" (vv. 26–28). Here we see more information about the new relationship to come: the disciples will pray directly to the Father; no longer do they need to rely on Jesus to ask for them. And that direct relationship is made possible by the love of God for each disciple and by the love of the disciple for Father God.

If you haven't recently read John 17, take a moment to read this chapter. It records Jesus's prayer for His disciples, committing them to God. Here Jesus models a deep commitment to prayer, communicating with His Father, expressing His desires, discussing His mission, seeking God's glory and strength for the coming trial, pronouncing God's truths about eternal life, and asking God to protect His twelve children and the future generations of spiritual children who will come through their witness.

As we prepare our children for graduation into the world, we must emphasize their communication with God. Jesus did this with urgency and consistency. Our Lord modeled a deep prayer life, letting the disciples hear His own prayers. Our emphasis on prayer does two things for our children.

We Point Them to God

As we teach our children to pray, we remind them that their ultimate source of direction is God the Father, through their relationship with Jesus Christ. Because parents will cease to be immediately present, our children will need God's guidance more than ever.

We Become a Resource Not a Dictator

Because we model our dependence on God through prayer, our children will know that we are here to help them by praying for them and seeking God's wisdom for them. We will not make their decisions for them, as a dictator would for his subjects. They must learn to discern God's will for themselves and then develop the courage to obey.

When Jesus encouraged His disciples to pray, He was encouraging direct communication with the heavenly Father. Because He soon would ascend to Heaven, Jesus also set the stage for continued communication between Himself and His disciples. In the same way, by encouraging our children to develop a strong prayer life, we encourage both prayer to God and a continuing line of communication with us as brothers and sisters in Christ. Here are four hints to help you encourage the prayer habits of your older teenage children. As you do these you will also be building a basis for subsequent communication with them.

1. MODEL A COMMITMENT TO PRAYER

Cultivate and nurture a prayer life yourself. It need not be perfect, only genuine. If you are struggling with this part of your life, be honest with your children. Pray in front of your children that God will help you develop the kind of prayer life He wants.

If you want your children to pray for a few minutes a day and then ignore God the rest of the day, it is easy enough to model, since that is common among Christian adults. On the other hand, if you want them to go to God continually, then model that by making prayer a vital part of your day—speaking to God about the big and little things that come up throughout the day. Teach your children that prayer is not only asking for stuff, but also involves hearing God and making the changes in our lives that He wants us to make. My best prayers have always been the ones that God changed while I was praying them. I thus got to see what God wanted me to pray, and then I got to observe Him answer that "improved" prayer.

2. MODEL A COMMITMENT TO HEAR YOUR CHILDREN

When your children are talking to you, make eye contact. Turn off the distractions. For me, I had to turn off the football games on TV. That was a struggle. Learn the best times to hear your children. Most teens go through periods when they won't talk at all to parents, and then there come those transmission bursts, where they are in a good mood and talk a lot. My wife has had the privilege of working at home, and tells me that right after school is usually a good time to hear about the kids' day. Teens will go through communication blackouts, so be ready when the blackout is lifted.

Determine to listen even when your teen is in an argumentative mood. They need to learn how to express contrary opinions to yours, and do so in a civil manner. This skill does not come easily. Even though you may have all the right facts and answers, let your children fully explain their points of view. Hold off giving them the killer argument that will slam-dunk your point. You may win the battle but ultimately cut off the line of communication.

3. Encourage Your Children to Get Answers from God

If the guidance they need is in the Bible (and it probably is), point them to the Book of the Ages. Encourage your children to pray about their issues, and remember to ask them if they got answers. Encourage them to bring up the issue in their Bible study class or with another Christian leader you both trust. Give your opinion when asked or when it is clearly necessary. Remember that you are trying to shift your child to get their answers without you. If the advice they get, even from other Christians, is not biblical or clearly not God's will for your child, as you discern it to be, then intervene. Until your child leaves your house or stops depending on your support, you retain the responsibility to set rules of behavior. For example, until age twenty-one, drinking alcohol is not legal in our state, and we let our kids know how we felt about drinking while at college. Other decisions, like who to ask to be a roommate, were not so black or white, so we gave them more latitude in these kinds of decisions.

4. Let God Speak to Your Children, Even If His Answer Is Uncomfortable

Oooh! This is hard. As parents, we have spent many years determining what is best for our children. Now we have to train ourselves to let God speak directly to them and to discern whether what our children are hearing is truly from God. If it is, we need to be prepared to let God lead. My experience is that if God is speaking to our children, He will be speaking the same message to us. Our job is to listen to God and be willing to set aside our human wisdom, if necessary.

Successful Communication

Like most parents, we struggled to communicate wisely with our children. One day our college-aged daughter asked if she could spend a year in France learning the language and increasing her understanding of European politics. While I wanted to weigh in immediately with my own opinions, I managed to hold my tongue long enough to hear her heart and gain her perspective on the benefits of her plan. By allowing her to talk uninterrupted through all the positives, she also began to lay out the negatives to being gone for a year. I would have been glad to list all those negatives for her, but because I listened and did not interrupt, she proved to be much more willing to consider the negatives fully, because she had come up with the list.

If I had jumped in to oppose her initial suggestion, she would have felt compelled to argue for going away, if only to prove that she could make her own decisions. The negatives would have been someone else's ideas (mine) and only the positives would have represented her position.

Other times I have been unwise, blasting in with my negative comments before my children had time to consider the negatives for themselves. I have been most successful when I listened, held my tongue, and challenged my daughters to pray for God's guidance. This strategy has never failed us.

In the above example, our daughter came back a week later saying she felt God was closing the door on the year-long program and that He had some other things for her to do. I knew that if God had led her to the year-long study program, none of our arguments would have mattered. I avoided becoming an impediment or, worse, an enemy, while preserving my position as a trusted counselor, and I was able to see God direct my child far more wisely than I could.

A friend shared an interesting listening technique with me recently. She'd heard of a mom who had the habit of butting in to solve her children's problems. Mom wised up finally, but found it so hard to keep quiet, she would keep a banana handy and eat it to keep her mouth occupied while she listened to her children. This proves that fresh fruit is healthy!

What Jesus Taught About Prayer
- The privilege of prayer—a direct line to the Father.
- Persistence in prayer—trusting God's timing.
- The promise of answers—God listens.

- The proper concerns of prayer—relationship with God and unity with others.

Chapter Eighteen
While Satan Tells Us To Be Consistent, God Prepared His Children for Change

When Sally received her schedule for the new semester, she noticed that Dr. Smith was the teacher for New Testament Greek. She was not excited.

The old seminary professor was not known for his cutting-edge teaching skills. In fact, Sally had heard that his primary teaching style was the old-fashioned lecture. Boring! In spite of her reluctance, Sally walked into the classroom on the first day of class and within minutes knew she was in for an interesting day. Dr. Smith had obviously gotten the hint from students' feedback that his teaching style needed some updating, so he had prepared an interesting icebreaker activity to start the semester.

On the wall hung a big paper target, and on a nearby table were many darts. The professor told the students to draw a picture of someone they disliked or someone who had made them angry, then he would allow them to throw darts at the person's picture. Sally's girlfriend drew a picture of a girl who had stolen her boyfriend. Another friend drew a picture of his stepbrother. Sally drew a picture of a former friend, putting a great deal of detail into her drawing, even drawing pimples on the face. Sally was pleased at the overall likeness she had created for her old "pal."

The class lined up and began throwing darts. Laughter and hilarity filled the normally subdued classroom. The first couple of students timidly threw their darts, but as the group warmed to the occasion, darts flew with such force that their targets began shredding. Although she felt a little juvenile for doing so, Sally actually looked forward to her turn. She was disappointed when Dr. Smith announced that because of time limits, the students needed to return to their seats.

As Sally sat stewing about her missed opportunity to throw darts at her target, Dr. Smith removed the tattered target from the wall.

Underneath the target was a well-known painting of Jesus's face.

An icy hush fell over the room as each student viewed the mangled face of Jesus. Holes and jagged marks marred His picture. His eyes were pierced.

Dr. Smith spoke quietly, "In as much as you have done it unto the least of these my brethren, you have done it unto Me."

Silence blanketed the room. Sally would never again see the face of her old enemy without also seeing the face of Jesus.

This wise college professor learned some new tricks and made adjustments to his teaching style. Jesus was a master teacher, and He, too, adjusted His approach as His disciples neared their launch date.

Jesus Introduced the Holy Spirit

Though Jesus in the flesh would soon be leaving the earth, He promised to be present in a new way: through the Spirit of God, who would not only be *near* His disciples but would actually be in them. Jesus said in John 16:7, "It is to your advantage that I go away; for if I do not go away, the Helper will not come." As good as it was to have Jesus among them, a new and better resource was on the way. How could this be? What could be better than having Jesus the miracle worker walking and working among them?

Let me ask a related question. What could be better for our children than to have us, their parents, right there with them in college? Imagine sitting in the seat beside your kid in English 101. You could answer the questions on the test that he couldn't get right or meet with the professor to get his grade changed. How about looking over her shoulder at her place of work? I could stand right beside my daughter, helping her get the customer's buffalo wing order written down right, then head home with her to balance her check-book every night. Ridiculous, isn't it?

There comes a time in every child's life that he or she must live independently, away from our guiding oversight. But that doesn't mean they won't take a part of us with them. And that's what Jesus was preparing the disciples for in John 14. Each of the following passages points to this preparation.

"I will ask the Father, and He will give you another Helper, that He may be with you forever, that is the Spirit of truth" (v. 16). The disciple does not earn this new presence; it is a gift as a result of Jesus's prayer. Also, this new presence will abide forever. Thus, it is clearly not a human presence, subject to separation common between human companions. And finally, this presence comes as a Helper, not a nag. He comes to strengthen, not drag down. This presence is the Spirit of truth, provided to help the disciples know right from wrong, truth from error. Thus, just as Jesus left the disciples but provided a universal presence, your kids will be separated from you but will take along those habits and heart attitudes you built into them.

"If anyone loves Me, he will keep My word; and My Father will love him, and We will come to him and make Our abode with him" (v. 23). The Holy Spirit, united with Jesus and God the Father, makes His home with the believer. Jesus made sure the disciples knew that the strength of the relationship between them would be determined by their choices in the future. If the disciples would keep Jesus's word—obey Him—they would find their relationship strengthened. If our children elect to sever the relationship with us, to ignore our teaching, they have the freedom to do so. We cannot stop them. This is the gut-wrenching truth of parenting. Our children can choose to suppress and turn away from the things we teach them. God has given them the dignity of a free will. But the free will decision to honor parents strengthens the relationship and gives our children many benefits.

"These things I have spoken to you while abiding with you. But the Helper, the Holy Spirit, whom the Father will send in My name, He will teach you all things, and bring to your remembrance all that I said to you" (vv. 25–26). Jesus promised that this new presence would continue to teach all things (even what Jesus could not teach in His three short years) and help us call to memory what we may have once known.

What are the implications for parenting? First and most obvious is that we must pray for our children to become Christians so that they will have the Holy Spirit residing in them. Parents must do all they can under God's guidance to lead their children to Christ. Second, parents need to teach their children about the Holy Spirit. Wise parents learn to rely on the Holy Spirit and help their children live daily in communication with Him. We need to help our children learn to hear the Holy Spirit. Third, parents need to relax. Their Christian children are in good hands.

But there is a less obvious implication. On the human plane, we instill a set of values in our children, for better or worse. These values form an inner resource that our children will call on when questions of right and wrong present themselves. We must challenge our children to recognize and appreciate their values, for soon those values will be challenged by a cynical professor or a sizzling temptation. If the values your children carry are not imbedded in their hearts, they will be shed like a down jacket in a heat wave. How can we find out what our children's values are?

- Watch what they choose to do when a friend hurts them.
- What do they buy with their money?
- How do they use their free time?
- How do they behave when they are angry?
- Do they seek forgiveness when they hurt someone?
- How do our sons treat the girls they know?
- How do our daughters treat boys?

With each day's trials and temptations, we gain insight into our children's value systems. Remember that values are modeled, so if you are not seeing what you want to see in your children, maybe you should examine your own values first. But there are times when, in spite of our best modeling and teaching, our children will act like, well, children!

Parents certainly do not instill the Holy Spirit in their children—only God can do that. And because of that, no child is hopeless. God can change a person from a disaster to a disciple, as He did me. One of our key tasks in preparing children for exit from our homes is to remind them of the presence of a Holy Spirit, who lives inside them (if they are a Christian), or wants to live inside them (if they are not). We can remind our Christian children that there will be guidance from within about what movies to see, what courses to take, what friends to keep, what girls or guys to date, and what clothes to wear. In short, we have a Helper for every need, but their job requires listening closely for that still small voice.

One important truth to share with our children about the Holy Spirit is that no godly urge is produced by our human nature. Paul put it this way: "Nothing good dwells in me, that is, in my flesh" (Rom. 7:18). Every urge to be more like Christ comes from the Holy Spirit, so we can set our compasses by His character. Conversely, if something draws us away from Christ, it is not a product of the Spirit. Knowing this truth deep down helps our children discern right from wrong.

A final truth to share is one of the best: You can be confident in this new resource. In Matthew 10:18–20, Jesus said, "And you will even be brought before governors and kings for My sake, as a testimony to them . . . do not worry about how or what you are to say; for it will be given you in that hour what you are to say. For it is not you who speak, but it is the Spirit of your Father who speaks in you." When your mouth gets dry and the spotlight is on you, the Spirit inside you will surface, and the Spirit will speak. Our children need to know that.

Jesus Shifted to a New Relationship
Wrapped up in Jesus's last instructions concerning prayer and the Holy Spirit is a tender exchange captured in John 15:13–15. In the upper room, Jesus addressed His friends, and His tone grew intimate. "Greater love has no

one than this, that one lay down his life for his friends. You are My friends if you do what I command you. No longer do I call you slaves, for the slave does not know what his master is doing; but I have called you friends, for all things that I have heard from my Father I have made known to you."

Think of it! The Creator of the universe chose to be our friend. He made us more than servants and more than students. More, even, than children. Jesus chose to treat His disciples as friends, opening Himself to them with total honesty. But with that friendship came a price. Because we became His friends, His enemies became our enemies. He said so in verses 19–20: "If you were of the world, the world would love its own; but because you are not of the world, but I chose you out of the world, because of this the world hates you.. . . If they persecuted Me, they will also persecute you."

On the basis of this friendship, Jesus warned the disciples of persecution. Our children need to be warned also. If they adopt Christ's values, and if they live out those values, they will run counter to the weave of our decaying society. The world will tell them to party hard, to grab every pleasure, even if a spouse is likely to get hurt. The world will tell them to fill their eyes with graphic images of sensuality, because, after all, you only live once, right? When Christians choose to abstain from sex outside of marriage, or to live within our means while our peers go into debt, we make peers' bad choices more obvious to them, and that creates tension. Even though we say nothing to condemn them, they feel uncomfortable. We must teach our children that life can be very uncomfortable. If our children adopt the values of the God of the Bible, they must be ready to make some tough choices. If they choose to pray, to be led by the Holy Spirit, they will be led where the unbelieving world will not go. But along the way, they will be the friends of Jesus Christ, and that's worth the sacrifice.

As parents, we must determine to treat our children as friends. For some of you, alarm bells are going off, because parents acting like school chums to their children conjures up images of forty-five-year-olds trying to act ridiculously hip. That's not what I mean, so let me explain. On the issues where our children must make independent decisions, we must treat them with the respect of a friend. When Jesus called His disciples friends, He did not stop being their Lord and Teacher. Instead, He told His friends the whole truth about the world, giving them information about His plans, His coming suffering, and the lowdown about the trials they would face. He respected the disciples enough to treat them as adults. They would make mistakes, and they would even desert their Lord that very night. Yet Jesus loved them and trusted them enough to share His most intimate thoughts with them. In the garden of Gethsemane, Jesus asked for their prayer support. He shared His fears and His anguish with them, and even took the closest of His disciples deeper into the garden to pray for strength.

There will come a time to be open and transparent with our children about our adult struggles with sin. This openness reveals our sincerity, and it models a practical humility before God that is attractive to our children. You must be wise to know when this time has come, for it is only proper when our children are ready to go out on their own.

For me, this time came around our daughters' last year

at home, or maybe even their last summer. As each daughter prepared to move off for college, I wrote a letter telling them how proud I was of them, and reminding them that my desire for them was related to "goodness" more than "greatness." I reminded them that I had been in the same place once, and that I had not made consistently wise choices during my college years. I left out the graphic details of those mistakes, but I was honest enough to assure them that they could bring their own failures to me, and we would both go to the heavenly Father for help.

As we broaden our relationships with our children, we never leave behind our role as parents. In fact, we become better able to influence our children, if they know that our advice, prayers, support, and hopes are based on the will of God. His will is unique to the child and each child must find it for him- or herself. We give our children to a big God, and He is able to take care of them.

Home Activities for Adapting Your Parenting

1. Ask yourself if you are willing to give up some author-ity and let your older teen children make some decisions for themselves. What are your biggest fears? What are you not willing to allow your child to choose while they still live at home? It's right and proper to enforce rules for your own home. For example, the summer after our daughters' senior year, we gave them a much later curfew for cer-tain occasions, but with plenty of discussion about being courteous to us as parents. We still wanted to know what, where, when, and with whom. We suggested that this was a chance to show us that they were mature enough to go off to college, so they knew their decision making was under scrutiny.

2. Obtain and go through a career assessment tool with your teen. Resources for this process are available through Crown Financial Ministries (Crown.org). This tool ad-dresses more than just academic skills. It touches on workplace preferences, human relationships in the mar-ketplace, and spiritual gifts.

3. If you haven't already, pray consistently for your child. A wonderful book to help give you structure and inspira-tion for this task is *The Power of a Praying Parent* by Stormie Omartian.

4. Seniors (twelfth graders) in our church go through several self-discovery tools to identify their spiritual gifts, talents, and personality types. This comprehensive

approach helped our kids set their sights on their personal ministry opportunities during the college years, and it provided an occasion for discussions about their gifts, talents, and personality types.

Deception 10:
Life Should Be Easy

Chapter Nineteen
Sheltered or Sent?

Some parents spend every resource to make their children's lives easy. But no matter how much padding we put around our kids, they suffer hurts of varying degrees. In an affluent society, we can sometimes fool ourselves into thinking that life is supposed to be easy. Satan spends a lot of his time on this particular lie, because those who believe it inevitably become discouraged. They even blame God for shattered hopes or for difficulties and walk away from His fellowship. Christian parents can fall for this lie just like the rest of the world does.

This lie blinds us when we think that this life is all-important. Jesus often said that this life is trivial in comparison to the life we will have in heaven (Matt. 5:11–12). Jesus told His followers to expect ill-treatment in this world, but He also reminded them that He had overcome the world. He told us that our rewards would far surpass the difficulties we face in this world. So the truth is, life is hard but the mission is worth it. Will we believe Jesus, or will we believe Satan? Will we shelter our children, or will we send them?

Sending Your Children Into a Code Orange World

As I write, the moving band of words on the news channel silently flashes that we live under a level orange terror alert. While parents are privileged to watch their grown children discover their unique role in God's plan, this privilege comes with a certain level of terror. Mine is at least orange, maybe red. Two of my daughters are considering a mission trip to Africa, and the possibility of encountering danger there is real. I have a certain amount of influence still with these very independent young women. But will I go with my gut, my level orange terror, or will I trust God to take them where He has been leading them all their lives? (Once I check with my wife, I'll let you know.)

It must have been hard for God to let Jesus go to the cross, for no amount of divinity could eliminate the pain of knowing your Son will suffer. But to our great gain, God didn't just allow Christ to go, He sent Him. There's a world out there that needs us, and God hears their cries. His loving response is to send Christian witnesses to the lost world, and your Christian children are in line for the job. It's not a matter of *if* they'll get an assignment; it's when. So my advice to you is to get used to an elevated terror level.

The challenge of this book is not just for you to let your children go out into the world; my message is to prepare them and then send them. Send them out armed with that strong foundation of relationship you formed with them. Your unconditional love is their introduction to God. Send them out with a tank full of memories of your presence in their lives. Send them out with a mental imprint of your genuine life in Christ modeled before them, disciplined in love and taught by your wise words. Send them out clothed with the experience of your family's mission and passion.

And finally, send them out armed with an active prayer life and the knowledge of the Holy Spirit. The best news is that if they have the Holy Spirit, He won't be content just to give them knowledge. He'll go with them, in the secret compartment of their hearts.

Jesus described the disciples' mission while He prayed for them: "As You sent Me into the world, I also have sent them into the world" (John 17:18). If you made Christ your Lord, you too were sent into this world with a mission. Your children, if they made Christ their Lord, leave your home with that same mission. This makes us, parents and children, comrades-in-arms. Your children will, in normal circumstances, leave the shelter of your home. Your only choice is whether you will send them out prepared, or simply let them go.

As followers of Christ, we all continue the mission of Christ, whom the Father sent into the world to redeem, to bring light to the blind, to set the captives free, to heal the sick. If we are on His mission, we will be less concerned about our fame or fortune than with helping those in need. And the greatest need of a world dead in sin is spiritual life. The greatest disciple training most of us are called to do is with our own children. Satan makes this job difficult by hiding God's parenting principles behind a pack of lies. Satan has been lying to us ever since our first parents roamed the garden of Eden. I'm tired of his lies. They are old, but truth is older still. In fact, He's eternal!

I am the way, the truth, and the life.

Jesus

Home Activities For Sending

1. When things go wrong for your child, you have an opportunity to help them process God's involvement in the difficulty. In the midst of suffering, avoid sermonizing. That's what Job's friends did, and God rebuked them. But later, when your child achieves some emotional distance from the disappointment, you can share with them how you hurt for them. You can share how your faith in God is tested but not destroyed. It's always good to ask God to reveal His plan within the disappointment. Sometimes He will. Always His Word stands ready to help us through the event. Other times God is silent so we can learn to trust Him through the pain.

2. Comfort your spouse as your children leave home. Empty nests are scratchy. Make sure you minister to one another in this time, and stay close to God. There will be ups and downs as your child finds both success and failure in life. God is mighty to save, and your child is in His view. Have fun. Your child will enjoy coming home to see you much more if your home is a place of happiness—if you are happy. If your child spends some time as a prodigal, don't lose hope. You can't take all the credit if they do well, so don't take all the blame if they struggle.

Appendix A

Secular Research: The Primacy of Relationship

A study of parenting styles makes clear that relationship is the key ingredient in raising "good" kids. This study examined the parenting behavior within numerous parent-child couplets. Two key characteristics were rated for each parent observed in the study: Emotional Warmth versus Emotional Coldness, and Strictness versus Permissiveness. Thus, the researchers categorized parents in one of four categories (Figure 1):

1. Authoritative—High Emotional Warmth and Strict
2. Indulgent—High Emotional Warmth and Permissive
3. Authoritarian—Low Emotional Warmth and Strict
4. Uninvolved—Low Emotional Warmth and Permissive

Figure 1. The Four Parenting Styles

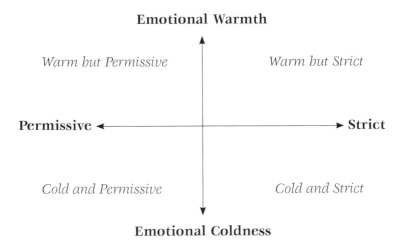

Results showed that one group of children were better adjusted than the other three groups. Which one? The children in the upper right quadrant, raised by emotionally warm but strict parents, were higher achieving and better behaving children. Now in some circles, this would be a big surprise, because many people think that strictly enforced rules will drive kids away and create distance between parent and child. Not so according to researchers. On the contrary, what children experience through tangible rules established for their own good *confirms* the emotional warmth that good parenting provides.

Which group was least well-adjusted? The children in the lower left quadrant, whose parents were cold and permissive, felt loved the least, not only due to a frigid emotional response from parents, but because of the absence of rules that proves a parent's love. In extreme cases of cold permissiveness, children become sociopaths, incapable of feeling sympathy and capable of tremendous cruelty to others.

E. E. Maccoby, and J. A. Martin, "Socialization in the Context of the Family: Parent-child Interaction," *Handbook of Child Psychology*, 1983, 44, 1–101.

Quoting from the article by Martin and Maccoby:

To summarize what has been presented concerning authoritarian parenting, a number of child characteristics have proved to be correlated with this pattern of parenting. Children of authoritarian parents tend to lack social competence with peers: thcy tend to withdraw, not to take social initiative, to lack spontaneity. Although they do not behave differently from children of other types of parents on contrived measures of resistance to temptation, on projective tests and parent reports they do show lesser evidence of "conscience" and are more likely to have an external, rather than internal, moral orientation in discussing what is the "right" behavior in situations of moral conflict. In boys, there is evidence that motivation for intellectual performance is low. Several studies link authoritarian parenting with children's low self-esteem and lack of internal motivation.

Appendix B

A Catalog of Jesus's Teachings in His Later Ministry

From Luke 9:23 to His Arrest

The episodes of teaching are coded to help you follow this listing. For example, Christ's teachings on the cost of discipleship (A) is the most common theme during Jesus's final months of life on earth, occurring in seventeen verses or passages.

CODE	TOPIC	# OF PASSAGES
A	Cost of discipleship	17
B	Prioriity of humility, thankfulness, devotion	15
C	Persistence and preparation for battle	10
D	Events that reveal who God/Jesus is	10
E	Warnings	9
F	Confrontations	7

Chapter/Code/Topic
(Starting in chapter 9, verse 23):

9   A   "Take up thy cross"

    D   Transfiguration

    C   Rebukes the disciples who cannot cast out demon

    A   Jesus predicts His death

    B   Jesus teaches humility: "whoever receives this little child"

    B   Samaritan village rejection; James/John call down fire

    A   Lessons on the cost of discipleship

10   B   Seventy sent out

    B   Parable of the good Samaritan

    B   Mary and Martha

11 C The model prayer
   C Lessons on persistence in prayer
   C Spiritual warfare: " a house divided"
   B "Blessed is the womb that bore you"
   F Evil generation seeks a sign
   F Dines with Pharisee: "woe to you"

12 A Beware of hypocrisy: several teachings on persecution
   B Parable of the rich fool
   B Do not worry; lilies of the field
   C Prepares disciples for the long fight; being wise steward
   A Christ brings division; prepare for battle
   A Discern the time
   A Make peace with your adversary

13 A Repent or perish
   A Parable of the barren fig tree
   F Woman bent over for eighteen years
   E Teachings on heaven and hell
   F Hard teachings: first will be last; stands up to Pharisees
   E Jesus laments over Jerusalem

14 F Healings on the Sabbath
   B Take the lowly seat
   E Parable of the great supper
   A Leaving all to follow Christ
   A Value of salt is in its distinctiveness

15 D Three parables: lost sheep, coin, son

187

16　A　Parable of the unjust steward

　　E　Teaching on divorce

　　A　Rich man and Lazarus

17　E　Jesus warns of offenses

　　A　Servant works without glory: duty

　　B　Ten lepers cleansed: thankfulness

　　C　Direct teaching on life after Jesus ascends

　　C　Direct teaching on life at the end of the age

18　C　Parable of the persistent widow: prayer

　　B　Parable of the tax collector, Pharisee

　　B　Jesus blesses children

　　A　Rich young ruler

　　A　Jesus predicts death

　　D　Jesus heals blind man

19　D　Zacchaeus: "Son of Man has come to seek, save the lost"

　　A　Parable on stewardship

　　D　The triumphal entry

　　E　Jesus weeps over Jerusalem

　　F　Jesus cleanses the temple

20　F　Jesus's authority questioned: a trap question

　　F　Parable of wicked vinedressers: warnings about rulers

　　F　Battle of wits: coin of Caesar, wives at the resurrection

　　C　More warnings about the scribes

21 A Observing the widow's two mites
   E Jesus predicts destruction of temple, Jerusalem, final end
   A "Watch therefore and pray"

22 D Preparation for the Passover
   D Lord's Supper; Jesus longs for this Passover fellowship
   B Disciples argue; Jesus washes their feet
   E Jesus predicts Peter's denial: realistic confidence
   E Jesus gives last instructions
   D Gethsemane: Jesus's last prayer teaching before the arrest

From the Author

It can happen! A person's eyes can be instantly opened to truth, dissolving in days what had been years of blinding deception. Thanks to God's intervention, my eyes were opened just like that. And my earnest desire for you is that you accept Christ for who He claims to be so that your eyes, too, may be opened. I earnestly believe your spiritual condition will affect your parenting, which will, in turn, influence the most important issue in your children's lives—where they spend eternity.

So for this book's parenting advice to be of greatest benefit, you must determine your spiritual condition. Are you alive or dead? Those are the only two choices. And just being religious doesn't ensure spiritual life. Jesus once spoke to a powerful, wealthy, and deeply religious individual, telling him, "You must be born again" (John 3:3). So, too, must you. If you trust your own goodness to get to heaven (or you trust that your good works outweigh your bad), you not only have a misplaced trust, Jesus says you lack a spiritual pulse.

To settle this important matter, don't rely on me. Grab a Bible and read the following verses in succession from the New Testament book of Romans: 3:23; 6:23; 5:8; 10: 9–10. If you will "confess with your mouth the Lord Jesus," meaning that you consider Jesus your authority for living because He is alive and real, and if you will call on Him to save you, you will be "born again." Whether you have already done this, or you are not yet convinced, please continue to seek God. He promises that if you seek Him with your whole heart, you will find Him (Jeremiah 29:13).

190

Notes

1. Chip Ingram, *Effective Parenting in a Defective World* (Atlanta: Walk Through the Bible Ministries, Inc., 2003). Visit www.lote.org.

2. George Barna, *The Future of the American Family* (Chicago: Moody Press, 1993).

3. T. Berry Brazelton and Stanley L. Greenspan, *The Irreducible Needs of Children: What Every Child Must Have to Grow, Learn, and Flourish* (Boston: De Capo Press, 2001).

4. CBSnews.com. "Does Day Care Damage Your Child?" Washington, April 19, 2001.

5. Elizabeth Warren and Amelia Warren Tyagi, *The Two Income Trap: Why Middle Class Mothers and Fathers Are Going Broke* (New York: Basic Books, 2003).

6. On a theological note, it takes no great intellect to realize that man tarnished the image of God somewhere along the way, and this explains the presence of evil, even though God is good.

7. Divorce may be the most effective time-stealer ever invented. Studies show that ten years after the divorce, two-thirds of noncustodial fathers are totally absent from their children's lives. Judith Wallerstein, *Second Chances: Men, Women, and Children a Decade After Divorce* (Boston: Houghton Mifflin, 1996).

8. G. Smalley and J. Trent, *The Language of Love* (Colorado Springs: Focus on the Family Publishing, 1988).

Parenting
S E M I N A R

Host a live parenting seminar featuring Dr. James Dempsey, a trained presenter with the National Center for Biblical Parenting. The title of the seminar is **Cooperation, Consequences and Keeping Your Sanity** and is designed for parents of children ages 2 through 18. The creative teaching style and powerful strategies shared provide parents with practical tools they can use right away. They'll learn specific ways that parents can move from simple behavior modification to a heart-based approach to parenting.

*Dr. Dempsey also does a free **Family Ministry Consultation** with church leaders to help them engage parents more effectively in their ministry to families.*

76 Hopatcong Drive, Lawrenceville, NJ 08648-4136
Phone: (609) 771-8002 • Email: JimD@biblicalparenting.org
Web: biblicalparenting.org

Made in the USA
San Bernardino, CA
16 July 2014